Coastal Fishes
of New Zealand
An identification guide

NEW EDITION
Malcolm Francis

REED

Published by Reed Books, a division of Reed Publishing (NZ) Ltd, 39 Rawene Road, Birkenhead, Auckland 10. Associated companies, branches and representatives throughout the world.

ISBN 0 7900 0512 3

First published 1988
Reprinted 1993
Revised edition 1996, 1988

Printed by Kings Time Printing Press Ltd, Hong Kong.

Front cover: Golden snapper *(Centroberyx affinis)*, Three Kings Islands.
Back cover: Female red pigfish *(Bodianus unimaculatus)*
          and gorgonian sea fans, Poor Knights Islands.

Contents

For Maryann, Melissa and Cara

Acknowledgements

This book owes its existence to the studies made by many marine biologists over the last two centuries; they patiently recorded the shape, colour, behaviour and biology of the fishes they saw and caught. More recently, amateur divers and diving biologists have added much to our knowledge of coastal fishes.

I am grateful to the many people who provided unpublished information and comments on the text, including: Quentin Bennett, Mike Bradstock, Fred Brook, Peter Castle, Wade Doak, Graham Hardy, Geoff Jones, Mike Kingsford, Rudie Kuiter, Natalie Moltschaniwskyj, Rob Murdoch, Ned Pankhurst, Chris Paulin, Clive Roberts, David Schiel, Andrew Stewart, Rowan Strickland, Clare Ward and Kim Westerskov.

Many photographers made their slides available, enabling the best possible species coverage and illustrations. Photo credits are listed on page 66. Thanks also to Kelly Tarlton's Underwater World for allowing me to photograph some difficult species in the aquarium.

The National Institute of Water and Atmospheric Research and the Leigh Marine Laboratory of the University of Auckland provided access to excellent library and computer facilities.

Finally, I owe most to Maryann Williams, my friend, diving buddy, fellow underwater photographer, and wife. Without her support, encouragement and personal sacrifices this book may not have made it!

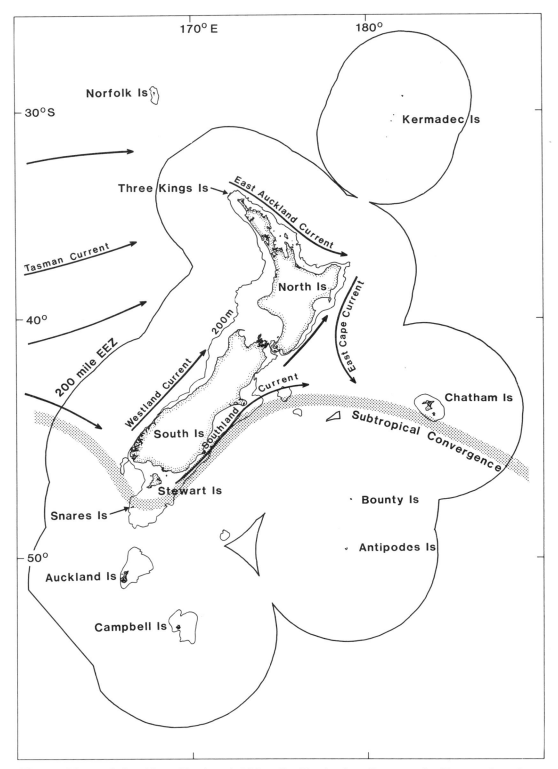

Fig. 1. Map of the New Zealand 200-mile Exclusive Economic Zone, showing the main ocean currents, outlying islands, and the 200-metre depth contour.

Introduction

From the Kermadec Islands in the north to the Campbell Islands in the south, New Zealand spans 2,600 kilometres of the Pacific Ocean. The main land masses are long and narrow, and the coastline is rugged and indented. All New Zealanders live close to the sea, so it is not surprising that we use it extensively for recreation and food. More and more people are learning to scuba dive as a way of exploring the sea. Divers are now able to observe and interact with marine life in its natural habitat, even if only for a short time.

Fishes are the most visible and striking of the sea's living inhabitants. Their abundance, colours, graceful movements and interesting behaviour attract attention. About 12,000 species of marine fishes are known worldwide, and around 1,100 of them have been found within New Zealand's 200-mile Exclusive Economic Zone. About 270 species occur in our shallow coastal waters, excluding oceanic migrants such as large sharks, marlins and tunas. However, some are restricted to remote islands; others are rare, well camouflaged, or occur in places divers rarely visit, such as estuaries. Consequently, many of our coastal fishes are unlikely to be seen by the average diver.

The main aim of this book is to provide a comprehensive guide to the fishes that divers are likely to see. It covers 127 species, including all the common reef fishes found between the Three Kings Islands and the Snares Islands. It also includes many of the rare fishes, and some which live over sand or mud bottoms. Many of the fishes that occur at the Kermadec Islands and the subantarctic islands are described, but some of the subtropical and subantarctic species which do not reach mainland New Zealand are omitted. For species which have different colour forms, or where the two sexes look different, each form is illustrated, and for some species distinct juveniles are shown as well.

All photos are of live fishes and were taken underwater. Most of the photos were taken using electronic flash, which restores the warm red and orange colours filtered out by seawater. Divers should remember that fishes seen in dim light or in deep water do not necessarily appear the same colour as shown in the photos. Colour *pattern* and body shape should still enable accurate identification of these fishes.

The text supplements the photos by highlighting the physical features, and for some species the behaviour, that make each species distinct. Details of geographic distribution, maximum length and habitat type are given for all species, and may also assist identification.

Another important aim of this book is to provide sufficient information about fishes to stimulate greater interest in them as living animals. We know what many of our fishes eat and how they catch their prey; we also know whether they are diurnal (active by day) or nocturnal, and often we have some idea of their growth rates and spawning seasons. Some species are hermaphrodites and may spawn first as females, then later as males. Many reef fishes live in the same small area for most of their lives, and may defend their territories. Information like this can add an extra dimension to diving, by helping to explain unusual observations.

I hope the information given here will answer some of the questions divers commonly ask. More importantly, I hope it will also arouse enough curiosity and interest that divers will actively *look* for various types of behaviour. For best results, you have to be patient and focus attention on one species at a time in one place — but the results can be rewarding. It will be obvious from the text that we know virtually nothing about some of our fishes,

so there is still great scope for amateur divers to make significant new discoveries.

If you see a fish that you cannot find in this book, it may be a very rare or even new species. If you see a fish outside the geographic ranges given here, you can add to our knowledge of its distribution. Readers are invited to contact me if they make any interesting observations, or would like help in identifying fishes. If possible, send a photo, drawing or even a specimen of the fish to make the job easier. Organisations with the expertise to help are the Museum of New Zealand and NIWA in Wellington, and the Auckland Institute and Museum. Other museums, university marine laboratories and Ministry of Fisheries regional offices can probably also help, or at least tell you who can.

Malcolm Francis
National Institute of Water and
Atmospheric Research (NIWA)
P.O. Box 14-901
Wellington

May 1996

Distribution of fishes within New Zealand

The wide latitudinal range of New Zealand's islands greatly affects the distribution of our fishes. The average summer water temperature ranges from about 24°C at the Kermadec Islands to about 9°C at the Campbell Islands. None of our coastal species occurs throughout this range of latitude, though blue moki (Kermadec Islands to Auckland Islands), sea perch and hapuku (Three Kings Islands to Campbell Islands) come close.

New Zealand is bathed by two major water masses — one subtropical and the other subantarctic (Fig. 1). Subtropical water extends from the Kermadec Islands to the Snares Islands, and subantarctic water occurs south of the Snares Islands. The two water masses meet at the Subtropical Convergence, a relatively narrow boundary zone where water temperature changes by several degrees. The position of the Subtropical Convergence varies seasonally, but it usually passes near the Snares Islands before turning north along the east coast of the South Island, and then east towards the Chatham Islands. In the far north, the Kermadec Islands are influenced by tropical water which moves southward during summer. These water masses influence the fish faunas found in different parts of New Zealand; the Kermadec Islands, for example, have a diverse subtropical to tropical fauna, whereas the subantarctic islands have a distinct subantarctic fauna. In mainland New Zealand, many coastal fishes range from the Three Kings Islands to Stewart Island, but they are not usually abundant throughout their range. Some species are distinctly northern (for example snapper, parore, red moki and kingfish) and decline in abundance towards the south; others are distinctly southern (for example girdled wrasse, telescopefish and sea perch) and decline in abundance towards the north. A few species, such as spotties and banded wrasse, are equally abundant throughout mainland New Zealand. (Surprisingly, spotties have not been seen at the Three Kings Islands or at the Snares Islands, though banded wrasse are abundant at both.)

This general pattern of fish distributions is modified by ocean currents. The offshore islands of eastern Northland and the Bay of Plenty support populations of a number of subtropical fishes that are very rare or

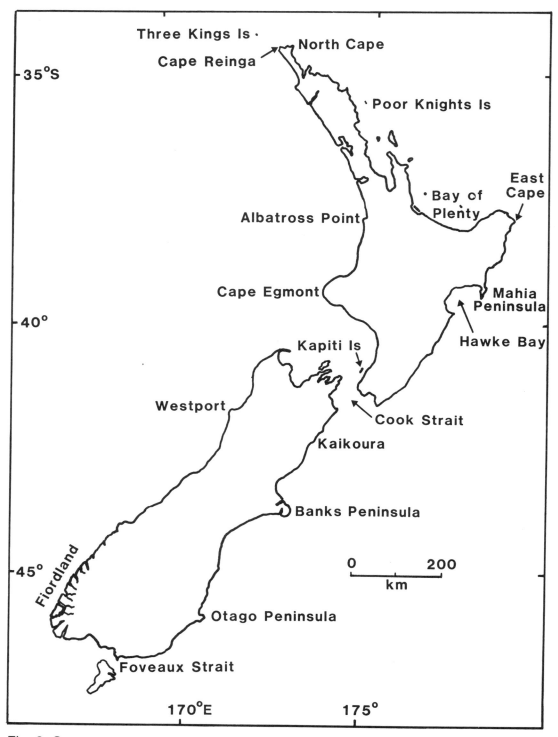

Fig. 2. Geographical localities used to describe fish distributions around mainland New Zealand.

absent elsewhere in New Zealand. The East Auckland Current flows southeast between North Cape and East Cape (Fig. 1), bringing clear, warm water (about 1–2°C warmer than on the adjacent mainland coast) to the offshore islands, and some of the mainland peninsulas and headlands (e.g. Cape Karikari, Cape Brett).

The East Auckland Current also transports larval and juvenile fishes to New Zealand from subtropical areas like Lord Howe Island and Norfolk Island. Some of these immigrant fishes do not survive the low water temperatures during their first winter here; others survive but are unable to reproduce, so their numbers decline steadily unless replenished by an influx of fresh larvae. Subtropical species tend to appear in New Zealand during particularly warm summers, and disappear during cold El Niño conditions. Many of the subtropical species that are rare around coastal headlands and offshore islands are abundant at the Kermadec Islands (e.g. orange wrasse, rainbowfish, toadstool grouper and gold-ribbon grouper).

The Three Kings Islands, situated northwest of Cape Reinga, are influenced by an upwelling of cold water from the deep layers of the Tasman Current, and their fish fauna is quite unusual for the latitude. Several common northern species (e.g. hiwihiwi, yellow moray and red pigfish) have not been recorded from the Three Kings, and several species more abundant in southern waters (e.g. blue moki, scarlet wrasse, common roughy) are often seen there. Girdled wrasse, which are otherwise known only from Hawke Bay southward, occur at the Three Kings. Other peculiarities include the absence of spotties and butterfish (the latter is replaced by the abundant blue-finned butterfish), and the presence of large numbers of crimson cleanerfish.

Many of the warm-water fishes common along the northeast coast of the North Island decline rapidly in abundance south of East Cape. The warm East Auckland Current flows mainly eastward at East Cape, though a branch flows south as the East Cape Current. The coast between East Cape and Cook Strait also receives cold-water pulses from the northward-flowing Southland Current. Thus, many northern species do not occur south of East Cape, though some straggle as far as Hawke Bay (e.g. yellow moray, pink maomao, Lord Howe coralfish and demoiselle). Some southern species (e.g. thornfish and southern pigfish) are not found north of East Cape, and others (e.g. trumpeter, warehou and copper moki) straggle northward in small numbers.

The west coast of the South Island is washed by the warm Westland Current and the east coast of the South Island is washed by the cold Southland Current. The cold-water notothenid cods (Maori chief, black cod and small-scaled notothenid) occur at the Snares Islands, Otago, and even as far north as Cook Strait, but so far have not been recorded from Fiordland. Conversely, sweep and goatfish have been seen in Fiordland but not off Otago.

The diversity of coastal fishes is greatest in the north, where subtropical species mingle with cooler-water species. Of the 127 species described here, 115 occur along the northeast coast of the North Island, but only about 50 are known from Fiordland. The diversity of coastal fishes at the subantarctic islands is very low — about 20–30 species occur there (including some not described in this book).

The fish communities of northern and southern New Zealand are quite different.

In the north, parore, silver drummer and marblefish are the main herbivores, and red moki and porae can be seen grubbing in the sediment on or near reefs for their food. In the south, butterfish and marblefish are the main herbivores, and blue moki, copper moki and tarakihi are the bottom-grubbers. Schools of trevally, koheru and jack mackerel may swirl around a northern diver, while a southern diver may be surrounded by telescopefish. At the Kermadec Islands and the subantarctic islands, fishes rare elsewhere in New Zealand may be the most abundant.

Family and species accounts

Species accounts form the main part of this book. They are designed to be used in conjunction with the colour plates to assist with the identification of fish species, and to provide information about their biology and behaviour. The information is presented under the following standard headings for quick reference.

Families

Species of fishes are grouped by scientists into *Families*, members of which share many features and are thought to have a common evolutionary history. Family names always end in '-idae'. The text under each Family heading consists of general comments on the size, behaviour and food of the species in that Family, and the number of species that occur in New Zealand coastal waters. For Families that have many New Zealand species, features common to all species are also described to avoid repetition in the species accounts.

Species

The species accounts are arranged alphabetically by scientific name within each Family.

Names

The first line of each species account consists of the common name(s), Maori name (if known), scientific name and plate number(s). Common and Maori names often vary regionally. The name given first is the name most commonly used in the region where the species is most abundant. Other widely used names are given in parentheses, but no attempt has been made to include all or even most of the known names.

Scientific names are in two parts: the first is the *generic* name and the second is the *specific* name. Every species has a unique combination of generic and specific names. Species belonging to the same genus, for example blue moki and copper moki, which belong to the genus *Latridopsis*, are very closely related. Red moki and painted moki, although superficially similar to blue and copper moki, are not very closely related to them and are placed in a different genus, *Cheilodactylus.*

There have been some recent changes to New Zealand fish names. This has resulted from closer study of the species, and comparison of specimens from New Zealand with those from overseas. If research shows

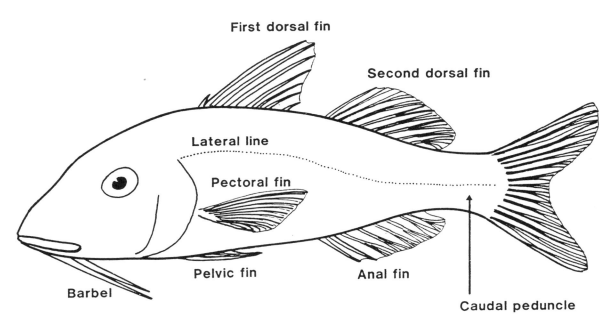

First dorsal fin

Second dorsal fin

Lateral line

Pectoral fin

Pelvic fin

Anal fin

Barbel

Caudal peduncle

Fig. 3. Diagram showing the technical terms used in the text to describe the various parts of a fish.

that two fish which had previously been thought to be different species are in fact one species, the older of the two names takes precedence. The names used here are the most recent, but there will undoubtedly be further changes as our knowledge of the species improves. Some New Zealand species have not yet been described by scientists and have no specific name, for example half-banded perch, *Hypoplectrodes* sp. ('sp.' is an abbreviation for 'species').

Identification

Most fish species that divers are likely to encounter can be identified by browsing through the photographs. The text supplements the photographs by describing each species' colour pattern and body shape; the main features are italicised for emphasis. In these descriptions, *bands* are vertical colour bars whereas *stripes* are horizontal bars. Patches of colour are referred to as *dots* (small), *spots* (medium) or *blotches* (large and often diffuse or irregular in shape). Terms used to describe the parts of a fish are shown in Fig. 3; see also the Glossary.

The approximate maximum length is given. This refers to the length from the snout to the 'V' in the tail for species that have forked tails; otherwise it is total length. Some species may grow longer than the lengths given here but most fish seen by divers will be considerably smaller.

If the species being described is likely to be confused with others, the differences among them are highlighted.

Distribution

The known distribution of each species in New Zealand waters is given, with the outlying islands (Kermadec, Chatham, Auckland, Campbell, Bounty and Antipodes Islands) being listed separately. The Three Kings Islands and Snares Islands are considered part of 'mainland' New Zealand in this book, because they lie on the same submarine plateau as the North, South and Stewart Islands. The subantarctic islands are defined here as those lying south of the Subtropical Convergence, i.e. Auckland, Campbell, Bounty and Antipodes Islands.

Many fishes are rare at the extremes of their distributions, and this is noted where known. Stray fish have a habit of appearing in the most unexpected places (e.g. spotted black grouper off Westport) but the distributions given will usually help you to decide whether an identification is likely to be correct. Areas where our knowledge of the fish fauna is poor are the coasts from East Cape to Cook Strait; from Cape Reinga to Cape Egmont; and from Farewell Spit to Jackson's Bay. Species that occur only in New Zealand are noted as *endemic*. Most non-endemic species also occur in Australia, or at Lord Howe and Norfolk Islands. A few species have worldwide distributions.

Habitat

Habitats occupied by each species are listed. Information on depth ranges is provided only where species are restricted to the upper or lower part of the depth range accessible to divers (0–50 m).

General

The amount of information about each species given in this section depends on how much is known. It may include food and feeding, swimming and schooling behaviour, night-time behaviour and colour changes, spawning and reproductive biology, growth rates, maximum known age, and whether the species is a subtropical immigrant. Information in this section may not always apply throughout New Zealand.

FAMILY MYXINIDAE: Hagfishes

Medium-sized, carnivorous, demersal, eel-like fishes without true jaws, bones or fins. One species occurs in coastal waters.

Hagfish (Blind eel, Tuere) *Eptatretus cirrhatus* **Plate 1**

IDENTIFICATION: *Body cylindrical with a paddle-like tail.* Six barbels around mouth. Pink-grey (but *appears blue-grey underwater*), variably spotted with black and white. *No eyes.* Length 80 cm.

DISTRIBUTION: Cape Reinga to Snares Islands; Chatham Islands. Most common south of Cook Strait.

HABITAT: Reefs and open bottom.

GENERAL: Hagfish prey on dead or live fish which they locate by smell and with their sensory barbels. They may catch prey at night, when many reef fish rest on the bottom. Hagfish suck on to their prey with their circular mouths, and rasp through the victim's flesh with their tooth-studded tongues. They escape predation themselves by exuding large quantities of mucus from a row of glands along each side of the body. Hagfish are probably hermaphrodites, maturing first as males and then changing sex to become females. They lay eggs enclosed in yellow-brown leathery cases.

FAMILY SCYLIORHINIDAE: Catsharks

Small, carnivorous, demersal sharks with two small dorsal fins towards the rear of the body. Most species lay eggs. One species occurs in coastal waters.

Carpet shark (Pekapeka) *Cephaloscyllium isabellum* **Plate 2**

IDENTIFICATION: Light brown with irregular dark brown saddles, spots and blotches. Length 100 cm.

DISTRIBUTION: Cape Reinga to Snares Islands; Chatham Islands. Most abundant in the south.

HABITAT: On or near reefs during the day, but may rove over sandy or shelly bottom at night.

GENERAL: Carpet sharks are nocturnal. During the day they rest in caves or under overhangs, where their camouflage makes them almost invisible. At night they roam widely in search of fish, krill, crabs, crayfish, octopus and squid which they catch and hold with their large mouths and sharp teeth. Carpet sharks are usually sluggish and are not dangerous, but their teeth deserve respect. As a defence against predators, they inflate their stomachs with air or water, greatly increasing their girth.

Carpet sharks lay eggs enclosed in tough leathery cases, about 12 x 4 cm. The egg cases, which are laid in pairs, are yellow or brown and have spiral tendrils at each corner for attaching to seaweed, sea fans or black coral. Eggs are fertilised internally by sperm transferred to the female by the male's claspers (visible in Plate 2, behind the pelvic fins). Young carpet sharks are about 16 cm long when they hatch from the eggs. Males mature at about 60 cm and females at 80 cm. Females grow larger than males.

FAMILY CARCHARHINIDAE: Requiem or whaler sharks

Medium to large sharks with the first dorsal fin large relative to the second, and a tail whose upper lobe is 2–3 times longer than the lower lobe. Most species give birth to live young. One species is seen regularly.

Bronze whaler shark (Horopekapeka) *Carcharhinus brachyurus* **Plate 3**

IDENTIFICATION: *Grey, brown or bronze above, white below. Large first dorsal and pectoral fins; long upper tail lobe.* Length 290 cm.

DISTRIBUTION: Cape Reinga to Cook Strait. Penetrates farthest south in summer.

HABITAT: All habitats in shallow coastal waters during summer — reefs, bays, estuaries and surf beaches. Possibly pelagic or offshore in winter.

GENERAL: Bronze whalers are opportunistic predators which will eat any live or dead animal material. They eat mainly fish, preferring schooling species (kahawai, pilchards, yellow-eyed mullet) and stingrays. Large prey are sliced up by the small, serrated teeth, assisted by vigorous head shaking. Bronze whalers rob fish from spearfishers, and although not usually aggressive towards divers they are potentially dangerous.

Bronze whalers mature at 220–250 cm, and females bear up to 23 young 60–70 cm long after a gestation period of about 1 year. As in all sharks, the eggs are fertilised internally; sperm are transferred to the female by the male's claspers.

FAMILY DASYATIDAE: Stingrays

Large, carnivorous, demersal rays with diamond-shaped bodies, no dorsal fins, and barbed spines on the tail. Two species occur in coastal waters.

Short-tailed stingray (Whai) *Dasyatis brevicaudata* **Plate 5**

IDENTIFICATION: Dark grey or black above with a *row of white spots (sometimes faint) along the wings; white underneath with broad grey margin. Tail the same length as, or shorter than, the body. Swims by undulation of wings.* Length 430 cm. Differs from the long-tailed ray (Plate 6) in tail length and in having white spots on the wings.

DISTRIBUTION: Kermadec Islands; Three Kings Islands to Foveaux Strait; Chatham Islands. Rare at the Kermadecs and south of Cook Strait.

HABITAT: Sandy or muddy areas such as harbours, estuaries and bays, but also frequently seen on reefs. Large groups may congregate in archways.

GENERAL: Short-tailed rays eat shellfish and crabs which they excavate from the sand or mud, possibly by the method used by eagle rays. Tail spines are used for defence only; stingrays are not aggressive towards divers, but are very dangerous if speared or stood on. The young are about 50 cm long at birth.

Long-tailed stingray (Whai) *Dasyatis thetidis* **Plate 6**

IDENTIFICATION: Dark olive green to black above *without white spots on wings;* white underneath. *Tail whip-like and up to twice the length of body. Swims by undulation of wings.* Length 400 cm. Differs from short-tailed ray (Plate 5) in tail length, and in lacking spots on wings.

DISTRIBUTION: Three Kings Islands to Cook Strait. Most abundant in the north.

HABITAT: Harbours and estuaries, usually in muddier areas than short-tailed rays. Occasionally seen on reefs.

GENERAL: The biology and behaviour of long-tailed rays are probably similar to those of short-tailed rays. The young are about 60 cm long at birth.

FAMILY MYLIOBATIDAE: Eagle rays

Large, carnivorous, demersal rays. One species occurs in New Zealand.

Eagle ray (Whai keo) *Myliobatis tenuicaudatus* **Plate 4**

IDENTIFICATION: *Wings pointed and head distinct. Swims by simultaneous, vertical flapping of wings.* Olive green, yellow or brown above with pale grey or blue markings; white underneath. One small dorsal fin and one or more barbed spines on tail. Length 200 cm.

DISTRIBUTION: Kermadec Islands; Three Kings Islands to Foveaux Strait. Rare at the Kermadecs and south of Cook Strait.

HABITAT: Most abundant over sand or mud, but frequently seen over reefs, or resting on sand patches within reefs.

GENERAL: Eagle rays are usually seen singly over reefs, but large numbers may congregate in shallow bays during summer. They have strong flat plates in both jaws which they use for crushing hard-shelled prey such as shellfish and hermit crabs. Only the meat is swallowed, and small piles of broken shells are left behind. Eagle rays also eat crabs, shrimps and worms. On soft bottoms, in search of their prey, they excavate steep-sided holes up to 20 cm across by taking in water through the large spiracles behind the eyes and jetting it out through the mouth or the gills. Eagle rays bear live young. Females grow faster and larger than males.

FAMILY MURAENIDAE: Moray eels

Medium to large, carnivorous, demersal eels without pelvic or pectoral fins, and with dorsal fins that start in front of the small gill opening. The skin is scaleless and covered in mucus. They have several rows of sharp teeth, some of which are hinged so that they fold backwards when prey is swallowed, but lock vertically if prey tries to escape. The array of teeth, and the opening and closing of the mouth required to oxygenate the gills, make morays appear aggressive. However, they are usually shy and are dangerous only if provoked. Morays are most active at night, and are usually seen in holes during the day.

Nothing is known about the reproduction and early life history of New Zealand morays, though they probably produce planktonic larvae. Seven species occur in New Zealand, but only five are commonly seen.

Mosaic moray *Enchelycore ramosa* **Plates 7 and 8**

IDENTIFICATION: *Dark brown with a mosaic pattern of cream blotches.* Jaws slender and unable to close fully. Length 180 cm.

DISTRIBUTION: Kermadec Islands; Three Kings Islands to East Cape. Mainly around offshore islands.

HABITAT: Reefs, in holes or crevices.

GENERAL: Mosaic morays eat crabs, fishes and possibly octopus.

Grey moray *Gymnothorax nubilus* **Plate 12**

IDENTIFICATION: *Grey with irregular brown markings.* Body and jaws slender. Dorsal fin high and usually edged in light blue or white. Eye white with a horizontal black stripe. Length 100 cm.

DISTRIBUTION: Kermadec Islands; Three Kings Islands to East Cape. Mainly around offshore islands.

HABITAT: Reefs.

GENERAL: Grey morays are seen in the open more frequently than other morays; they may drape themselves around kelp or sponges. They are also more active during the day, and eat crabs, shrimps and small fishes.

Speckled moray *Gymnothorax obesus* Plate 10

IDENTIFICATION: *Dark brown with closely spaced cream or fawn spots; eyes bluish.* Head and jaws short and stocky. Length 200 cm.

DISTRIBUTION: Three Kings Islands to East Cape. Most common around offshore islands, but frequently seen on the coast.

HABITAT: Reefs, in holes or crevices.

GENERAL: Speckled morays behave aggressively towards each other, so they are presumably territorial.

Yellow moray (Pūharakeke) *Gymnothorax prasinus* Plate 11

IDENTIFICATION: *Yellow,* often with a green tinge along the belly; eyes blue. Head and jaws short and stocky. Length 150 cm.

DISTRIBUTION: Cape Reinga to Hawke Bay.

HABITAT: Reefs, in holes or crevices.

GENERAL: Yellow morays are territorial and defend their territories aggressively against each other. They eat crabs, shrimps and small fishes.

Mottled moray *Gymnothorax prionodon* Plate 9

IDENTIFICATION: *Brown with white spots.* Head and body slender. Length 100 cm.

DISTRIBUTION: Cape Reinga to Mayor Island. Most common around offshore islands and coastal headlands.

HABITAT: Reefs, usually in holes or crevices, but also seen in the open.

GENERAL: Mottled morays eat crustaceans and possibly small fishes.

FAMILY CONGRIDAE: Conger eels

Medium to large, carnivorous, demersal eels with pectoral fins but no pelvic fins. The dorsal fin starts above or just behind the pectoral fin, and the skin is scaleless. Two species occur in coastal waters. They can be confused with freshwater eels (Family Anguillidae) which are occasionally seen in the sea, but the dorsal fin starts well behind the pectoral fin in freshwater eels.

Common conger eel (Ngōiro) *Conger verreauxi* Plate 13

IDENTIFICATION: *Blue-grey, sometimes paler below;* large eels may be nearly black. *Dorsal fin starts above rear edge of pectoral fin. Lips large and fleshy. Grows very large.* Length 220 cm. Differs from northern conger eel (Plate 14) in size, position of dorsal fin origin, and in lacking a black margin on the fins (except in small fish).

DISTRIBUTION: Three Kings Islands to Snares Islands; Chatham Islands. Most abundant from Cook Strait south.

HABITAT: Reefs, in caves and crevices.

GENERAL: Common conger eels are nocturnal, roving at night in search of fishes, crabs, crayfish and octopus. Males are generally smaller than females. Conger eels probably spawn only once and then die. The eggs develop into a large, planktonic, leaf-like larva which was once thought to be a different species.

Northern conger eel *Conger wilsoni* Plate 14

IDENTIFICATION: *Dark grey above, lighter below; black margins on dorsal and anal fins. Dorsal fin starts behind rear margin of pectoral fin.* Length 100 cm. Differs from common conger eel (Plate 13) in size, position of dorsal fin origin, and in having black fin margins.

DISTRIBUTION: Kermadec Islands; Three Kings Islands to Kaikoura.

HABITAT: Reefs, in caves and crevices.

GENERAL: The northern conger eel is nocturnal, and eats crabs, shrimps and small fishes. It probably spawns only once before dying.

FAMILY SYNODONTIDAE: Lizardfishes

Small, carnivorous, demersal fishes usually seen propped up on the bottom on their pelvic fins, or half-buried in sand. Their heads are lizard-like and their snouts are pointed. Two species occur in coastal waters.

Red lizardfish *Synodus doaki* **Plate 15**

IDENTIFICATION: *Alternating, wavy, dark red and light bands.* Length 25 cm.

DISTRIBUTION: Kermadec Islands; Cape Reinga to Poor Knights Islands. Rare. Usually seen around offshore islands.

HABITAT: Sand, cobbles, and occasionally reefs. Usually deeper than 25 m.

GENERAL: Red lizardfish probably eat crabs, shrimps and small fishes. They feed by lying motionless on the bottom, then launching themselves forward with gaping mouth to engulf any passing prey. Red lizardfish are probably subtropical immigrants that arrive in northern New Zealand as larvae during warm summers.

Lavender lizardfish *Synodus similis* **Plate 16**

IDENTIFICATION: *Fawn above, with several red-brown saddles; pale blue stripe along middle of body, beneath which is a row of red blotches; several black spots on upper gill cover.* Length 22 cm.

DISTRIBUTION: Cape Reinga to Poor Knights Islands. Rare.

HABITAT: Sand or cobbles, close to reefs.

GENERAL: Often seen in pairs. Feeding is probably similar to that of the red lizardfish. Lavender lizardfish are subtropical immigrants that arrive in northern New Zealand as larvae during warm summers.

FAMILY MORIDAE: Morid cods

Small to large, carnivorous, demersal fishes, many of which live mainly over soft bottom. Five species occur on coastal reefs, but only three are likely to be seen by divers.

Rock cod (Taumaka) *Lotella rhacinus* **Plate 17**

IDENTIFICATION: Uniform *fawn to dark brown; white or light blue margins on second dorsal, anal and tail fins. Tail rounded.* Length 40 cm. Differs from southern bastard cod (Plate 19) in having light fin margins; from red cod (Plate 18) in having a rounded tail and in lacking a black pectoral spot; and from a closely related species, *Lotella phycis* (not illustrated), in having smaller scales and growing to a larger size (*L. phycis* reaches only 18 cm).

DISTRIBUTION: Kermadec Islands; Three Kings Islands to Stewart Island; Chatham Islands.

HABITAT: Reefs, in caves and crevices. Usually deeper than 12 m.

GENERAL: Rock cod are nocturnal, emerging at night to feed on small fishes, crabs and shrimps.

Red cod (Hoka) *Pseudophycis bachus* **Plate 18**

IDENTIFICATION: *Copper, pink or grey above, white or pink below; large black spot at base of pectoral fin.* Tail has straight rear edge. Length 80 cm. Differs from rock cod (Plate 17) and southern bastard cod

(Plate 19) in tail shape and in having a black pectoral fin spot.

DISTRIBUTION: Cape Reinga to Snares Islands; Chatham Islands; all the subantarctic islands. Abundant south of Cook Strait.

HABITAT: All bottom types. In shallow water red cod are found in caves or under overhangs by day, and are active only at night. In deeper water they are active by day, often forming very large schools over sand or mud.

GENERAL: Red cod use the sensory barbel on the lower jaw to detect prey buried in sand or mud. Small fish (up to 25 cm) eat mostly invertebrates, whereas large fish eat a high proportion of fishes as well as large crabs and krill.

Red cod spawn in August–October in deep water over the edge of the continental shelf. Juveniles grow rapidly, reaching 25–30 cm after 1 year, and maturing at about 50 cm at 3 years. Few live beyond 7 years.

Southern bastard cod *Pseudophycis barbata*
Plate 19

IDENTIFICATION: *Grey-brown*, blotched with light grey or white. *Pectoral and tail fins rounded; second dorsal, anal and tail fins have black margins.* Length 65 cm. Differs from rock cod (Plate 17) in having black fin margins; from red cod (Plate 18) in having rounded tail and pectoral fins, and in lacking a black pectoral spot; and from a closely related species, *Pseudophycis breviuscula* (not illustrated) in having smaller scales and growing to a larger size (*P. breviuscula* reaches only 25 cm).

DISTRIBUTION: Three Kings Islands to Snares Islands; Chatham Islands. Most common from Cook Strait south.

HABITAT: Reefs, caves and under overhangs.

GENERAL: Southern bastard cod feed nocturnally on crabs, shrimps and possibly small fishes. They spawn during summer.

FAMILY HEMIRAMPHIDAE:
Halfbeaks

Medium, surface-schooling fishes with very long lower jaws. Two species occur in coastal waters but only one is common.

Piper (Garfish, Ihe) *Hyporhamphus ihi*
Plate 25

IDENTIFICATION: *Lower jaw much longer than upper,* and orange-tipped. *Dark blue-green above, silver and white below.* Length 40 cm.

DISTRIBUTION: Cape Reinga to Foveaux Strait; Chatham Islands. Endemic.

HABITAT: Forms schools just below the surface, in harbours and bays. Occasionally seen over reefs.

GENERAL: Piper are omnivorous. They eat eel grass and green seaweed, and also planktonic crustaceans, worm larvae and insects that land on the water surface. They detect the vibrations of their animal prey through the sensitive lateral line system in the lower jaw; with this system they are able to feed actively at night.

Piper spawn in early summer. Their eggs sink to the bottom and stick to seaweed or eel grass, where they remain until hatching. Piper mature at about 22 cm.

FAMILY TRACHICHTHYIDAE:
Roughies

Small to large, planktivorous, demersal or midwater fishes with large bony heads and large eyes. Some species have a row of bony scales along the belly. Two species occur in coastal waters.

Slender roughy (Puramorehu) *Optivus elongatus* **Plate 20**

IDENTIFICATION: *Slender, copper-coloured body,* paler above than below; *red-brown stripes on upper and lower tail lobes.* Length 12 cm. Differs from common roughy (Plate 21) and bigeye (Plate 22) in body shape, and in having tail stripes.

DISTRIBUTION: Kermadec Islands; Three Kings Islands to Cook Strait; Chatham Islands. Rare south of East Cape.

HABITAT: Reefs, in caves and crevices by day.

GENERAL: Slender roughies are nocturnal, emerging at night to feed on planktonic crustaceans. They often school with bigeyes, and share the same daytime retreat. Spawning probably occurs in summer, because juveniles 2–4 cm long appear on reefs in late summer.

Common roughy (Sandpaperfish, Patohe) *Paratrachichthys trailli* **Plate 21**

IDENTIFICATION: *Deep, copper-brown body,* paler below; all fins pink. Skin rough like sandpaper. Length 30 cm. Differs from slender roughy (Plate 20) in body shape, and in lacking tail stripes; and from bigeye (Plate 22) in body shape.

DISTRIBUTION: Three Kings Islands to Snares Islands; Chatham Islands. Uncommon north of Cook Strait. Endemic.

HABITAT: Reefs, in caves and crevices by day, though in deeper water they may be seen in the open during the day.

GENERAL: Common roughies are nocturnal in shallow water, emerging at night to feed on planktonic crustaceans and larval worms. They spawn in spring and summer.

FAMILY BERYCIDAE: Alfonsinos

Medium to large, planktivorous, demersal or midwater fishes. One species occurs in coastal waters.

Golden snapper (Koarea) *Centroberyx affinis* **Plate 23**

IDENTIFICATION: *Bright orange-red,* but may appear silver with an orange or red tinge in flash photos. *Tail strongly forked; large eyes* and mouth. Length 55 cm.

DISTRIBUTION: Kermadec Islands; Three Kings Islands to Foveaux Strait. Most abundant in the north; rare south of Cook Strait.

HABITAT: Reefs with caves, overhangs or canyons.

GENERAL: Golden snapper are nocturnal. During the day they hide in caves or under overhangs, except in deeper water where they school in the open. At night they form loose schools in midwater and feed on large plankton, such as crustaceans and small fishes.

FAMILY ZEIDAE: Dories

Small to medium, carnivorous, demersal or midwater fishes with deep, compressed bodies and highly protrusible jaws. One species occurs in coastal waters.

John dory (Kuparu) *Zeus faber* **Plate 24**

IDENTIFICATION: Silver, grey or light brown, with green-brown wavy stripes; *large, central black spot* ringed with silver. *Body very thin;* dorsal fin very high. Length 60 cm.

DISTRIBUTION: Three Kings Islands to Foveaux Strait; Chatham Islands. Rare south of Cook Strait.

HABITAT: Reefs, sand and mud. Near the bottom or midwater.

GENERAL: John dory swim by undulating their nearly transparent second dorsal and anal fins; the tail is rarely used and the body is kept rigid. This swimming mode allows them to stalk their fish prey unobtrusively, relying on their extremely thin bodies to make themselves almost invisible from the front. To take advantage of their prey's blind spot, they often stalk them from behind at an oblique angle. When several centimetres from their prey, the john dory shoots out its long mouth tube and swallows the victim whole. John dory eat a variety of fishes including small schooling species and larger reef fishes. They hunt by day and are usually solitary, but large aggregations, possibly associated with spawning, sometimes occur in midwater.

John dory spawn from December to April, with activity peaking in February–March. They grow rapidly initially, reaching 15–20 cm at the end of their first year. After that, females grow faster than males. Females mature at 35–40 cm and an age of 5 years, whereas males mature at 30–35 cm and 4 years. Females live up to 9 years, and grow larger than males, which live up to 7 years.

FAMILY SYNGNATHIDAE: Sea horses and pipefishes

Small to medium, carnivorous, demersal fishes with an external covering of ridged bony plates. Swimming ability is limited, and many species have a prehensile tail for gripping seaweed. Six species of pipefishes and one sea horse occur in coastal waters, though they are rarely seen because of their excellent camouflage.

Sea horse (Manaia) *Hippocampus abdominalis* Plate 26

IDENTIFICATION: *Distinctive shape* with prehensile tail, protruding belly and tube-like snout; males have long filaments on top of head. Colour ranges from light grey to almost black, but is *usually yellow or brown*

with darker spots on body and bands on tail. Length 35 cm.

DISTRIBUTION: Three Kings Islands to Snares Islands; Chatham Islands.

HABITAT: Harbours, bays and reefs.

GENERAL: Sea horses are usually found entwined around seaweed. They can swim slowly forwards in an upright position by fanning the small pectoral fins on the sides of the head; or they can swim more rapidly with the body stretched forward at an angle of 45° by beating the dorsal fin on the back. Sea horses eat small crustaceans which they find among the seaweed or in the plankton, sucking them into their mouths as if using a drinking straw.

Spawning occurs in spring and summer. Females deposit their eggs in a pouch on the male's belly. He fertilises them, and broods them until they hatch after about 30 days. The miniature sea horses are then ejected by muscular contractions of the pouch, or when the male compresses the pouch against a hard object. Up to 200 sea horses 1–2 cm long may be ejected at a time.

Spiny sea dragon *Solegnathus spinosissimus* Plate 27

IDENTIFICATION: *Distinctive body shape; covered in blunt prickles. Red-orange,* with some light blotches and many *fine yellow bands and dots;* red-brown patch on the belly. Tail slightly prehensile. Length 50 cm.

DISTRIBUTION: Cape Reinga to Stewart Island; Chatham Islands.

HABITAT: Reefs.

GENERAL: Spiny sea dragons anchor themselves to seaweed or sea fans while feeding on planktonic crustaceans. They are more mobile than sea horses and may be seen moving over open bottom.

The male sea dragon has no brood pouch (unlike the sea horse); instead the female attaches her eggs to the underside of the male's tail, just behind the anus. He carries the eggs until they hatch into miniature sea dragons.

FAMILY SCORPAENIDAE:
Scorpionfishes

Small to medium, carnivorous, demersal fishes with large spiny heads. Most species are sedentary, well camouflaged, and have venomous dorsal fin spines. Scorpionfishes fertilise their eggs internally, and give birth to live young. Three species are commonly seen in coastal waters.

Sea perch (Jock Stewart, Pohuiakaroa)
Helicolenus percoides **Plate 32**

IDENTIFICATION: Mottled brown and white, with *four red-brown bands on body, the third split near the top;* usually another brown band on nape, and a row of white dots running along lateral line. Length 45 cm.

DISTRIBUTION: Three Kings Islands to Snares Islands; Chatham Islands; Bounty Islands; Antipodes Islands; Campbell Islands. Most common south of Cook Strait.

HABITAT: Reefs or nearby open bottom.

GENERAL: Sea perch are usually seen lying on the bottom, propped up on their pectoral fins. They eat a wide variety of small fishes, crabs and shrimps which they catch with a rapid lunge as their prey passes close by. Sea perch give birth to live young; the larvae are extruded in a jelly-like mass which floats to the surface. The jelly dissolves quickly, leaving the larvae free in the plankton. The adults are ripe for much of the year so the spawning period is probably lengthy.

Northern scorpionfish (Matuawhāpuku)
Scorpaena cardinalis **Plate 30**

IDENTIFICATION: *Head and mouth very large.* Variably mottled with red, brown and white, basic colour changing with background. *Small white or silver spot in centre of body, usually preceded by larger red-brown blotch;* diffuse light blotch on back between dorsal fins; *rear of body banded, with prominent dark band below second dorsal fin,* followed by a light band, and another *dark band on caudal peduncle;* white spot at top of last dark band. Length 60 cm. Differs from dwarf scorpionfish (Plate 31) in size and colour pattern.

DISTRIBUTION: Three Kings Islands to East Cape.

HABITAT: Reefs.

GENERAL: Northern scorpionfish are nearly always seen resting on a rocky bottom, often in the open during the day. They are well camouflaged, being able to change their colour to blend in with the background. They eat mainly fishes, but also catch crabs, shrimps and octopus. During the day they catch prey by lunging at any unsuspecting animal which passes too close; the prey is engulfed by the large mouth and swallowed whole. At night, scorpionfish are more active, and probably rove around the reef in search of sleeping fish.

Northern scorpionfish may be aggressive towards divers, especially those who land on or near the practically invisible fish. They may butt or bite the diver, though their teeth are small and do little damage. However, a careful diver can approach scorpionfish very closely and get virtually no reaction.

Dwarf scorpionfish *Scorpaena papillosus*
Plate 31

IDENTIFICATION: *Very similar to northern scorpionfish (Plate 30) but lacks light spots on mid-body, back and caudal peduncle. Banding on rear of body is more irregular, and light-coloured scales have dark margins; light band (white, pink or mauve) often runs across nape and on to gill covers.* Length 25 cm.

DISTRIBUTION: Three Kings Islands to Snares Islands; Chatham Islands.

HABITAT: Reefs, usually in caves or crevices, or under overhangs.

GENERAL: Dwarf scorpionfish are nocturnal. Their small size, excellent camouflage and secretive behaviour mean they are seldom seen, though they are common. They eat crabs, hermit crabs and shrimps.

FAMILY CONGIOPODIDAE: Pigfishes

Small to medium, carnivorous, demersal fishes with long snouts and high dorsal fins. One species occurs in coastal waters.

Southern pigfish (Purumorua) *Congiopodus leucopaecilus* **Plate 28**

IDENTIFICATION: *Distinctive head profile, with high spiny dorsal fin. Light to dark brown, blotched with dark brown and white;* series of short, cream-white bands along middle of body. Length 40 cm.

DISTRIBUTION: East Cape and Kapiti Island to Snares Islands; Chatham Islands. Rare north of Cook Strait.

HABITAT: Shallow reefs, harbours and bays.

GENERAL: Southern pigfish are usually seen resting on the bottom, often nestled in seaweed or against rocks. Their camouflage colour, spiny dorsal fin and tough, leathery skin protect them from most predators, and they have little fear of divers, allowing them to approach closely and even to handle them. They eat crabs, worms and other small animals, catching them by sucking them out from among seaweed, or from under pebbles, with their long, protrusible jaws. Pigfish spawn during winter and spring.

FAMILY TRIGLIDAE: Gurnards

Small to medium, carnivorous, demersal fishes with a covering of strong bony plates on the head. The first three rays of their pectoral fins are modified as sensory feelers, and are also used for 'walking'. The rest of the pectoral fin forms a large, brightly coloured fan. One species occurs in coastal waters.

Red gurnard (Kumukumu) *Chelidonichthys kumu* **Plate 29**

IDENTIFICATION: *Fawn or pink above,* with sparse *orange or brown blotches;* silver below. First dorsal fin mostly orange or red; *pectoral fins olive green with turquoise margins and dots,* with large, white-dotted, black blotch near rear edge. Length 65 cm.

DISTRIBUTION: Three Kings Islands to Stewart Island; Chatham Islands.

HABITAT: Sand or mud.

GENERAL: Red gurnard 'walk' on the bottom using the sensory feelers on their pectoral fins. These feelers also scare prey into the open where they are snapped up. Crabs and shrimps are the main food, but small fishes and worms are also eaten.

The large pectoral fins are spread to give stability when swimming, but they are probably used mainly by gurnard displaying to each other, or for flashing open to scare off predators. Gurnard spawn in spring and summer. Juveniles grow quickly, some maturing at 2 years old, and all by 4 years. Females grow faster and bigger than males, maturing at about 33 cm, compared with 26 cm for males. Few live longer than 10 years.

FAMILY SERRANIDAE: Groupers

Small to large, carnivorous fishes which have two different types of lifestyle: some species are demersal predators which live singly, in pairs or in small groups, whereas others are schooling planktivores. Many of the predatory groupers are seen in caves or under overhangs by day, suggesting that they feed at night, or at dawn and dusk. Many (possibly all) groupers are hermaphrodites, having both male and female gonad tissue at some stage of their lives. Eight species are commonly seen in shallow coastal waters, and several others are rare.

Yellow-banded perch *Acanthistius cinctus* **Plate 36**

IDENTIFICATION: *Yellow with 6 black bands on body and black stripes radiating from eye;* fins (except first dorsal) grey, edged in black and white, and dotted with black. Length 60 cm.

DISTRIBUTION: Kermadec Islands; Cape Reinga to Great Barrier Island. Abundant at the Kermadecs but rare in New Zealand, where it occurs mainly around offshore islands.

HABITAT: Reefs, in caves and under overhangs.

GENERAL: Yellow-banded perch occupy the same area for months, so they are probably home-ranging. They occur singly, in pairs, or in small groups, and eat fishes.

Gold-ribbon grouper *Aulacocephalus temmincki* **Plate 37**

IDENTIFICATION: *Dark blue with broad gold stripe along back and snout;* narrow stripe along upper jaw. *Body very thin.* Length 40 cm.

DISTRIBUTION: Kermadec Islands; Cape Reinga to Poor Knights Islands. Abundant at the Kermadecs, rare elsewhere.

HABITAT: Reefs, in caves and under overhangs.

GENERAL: Gold-ribbon grouper hover in caves by day, presumably emerging to feed by night. Nothing is known of their biology. They are subtropical immigrants that arrive in northern New Zealand as larvae during warm summers.

Butterfly perch (Oia) *Caesioperca lepidoptera* **Plate 34**

IDENTIFICATION: *Light pink with large, central, black blotch* and numerous *brown and black spots;* head pink with iridescent blue markings around and behind eye. Length 40 cm.

DISTRIBUTION: Three Kings Islands to Snares Islands; Chatham Islands.

HABITAT: Forms schools which are never far from a rocky bottom. Often found near a reef or a pinnacle where current is strong.

GENERAL: Butterfly perch are planktivorous, eating mainly small crustaceans and salps which are carried to them by the current. At night they rest on the bottom, their colour changing to blotchy pink with the black blotch fading to grey. Butterfly perch spawn in pairs in July–October, and juveniles 2 cm long are found on the reef in November. They reach maturity at the end of their first year, at a length of 10 cm, and live up to 8 years.

Pink maomao (Mātātā) *Caprodon longimanus* **Plates 38 and 39**

IDENTIFICATION: *Bright pink* with red-orange markings on face, and light blue margins on fins. A rare colour variety has black markings on rear of dorsal fin and upper back, and lines of yellow spots on face and upper front part of body; all fins yellow except dorsal, and all have blue margins or blue tips except pectoral. Length 55 cm.

DISTRIBUTION: Kermadec Islands; Three Kings Islands to Hawke Bay. Most abundant around islands and coastal headlands.

HABITAT: Schools in midwater in areas of moderate current flow around islands, pinnacles and archways.

GENERAL: Pink maomao feed actively during the day on plankton and salps carried by currents. They occasionally feed at the surface, but are usually seen deeper than 10 m, often beneath schools of blue maomao and butterfly perch. At night they rest on a rocky bottom, their colour changing to a blotchy pink-red. The black-backed colour variety (Plate 39) has been found throughout the year, and in non-spawning fish, so it is not associated with spawning. Pink individuals are able to change into the black-finned colour variety, but the reason for this is unknown. Pink maomao probably spawn in winter.

Spotted black grouper *Epinephelus daemelii* **Plate 45**

IDENTIFICATION: Body colour varies from almost white to brown-black, and can change from one extreme to the other in seconds; dark fish appear blue-grey. *Five oblique, brown-black bands on body plus a darker saddle on caudal peduncle;* numerous white spots cover head and body; pelvic, anal, second dorsal and tail fins edged with black and white. Length 200 cm (rarely longer than 80 cm, except at the Kermadec Islands).

DISTRIBUTION: Kermadec Islands; Three Kings Islands to Cook Strait and Westport. Abundant at the Kermadecs, common at the Three Kings, but rare elsewhere.

HABITAT: Reefs, especially near caves, overhangs and archways. Usually less than 25 m deep.

GENERAL: Spotted black grouper are solitary or occur in small groups. They are home-ranging and may occupy the same cave or overhang for years. Fish over 100 cm long are strongly attracted to divers, but small fish are much more wary.

Spotted black grouper begin life as females and change sex at about 100–110 cm; therefore the largest animals are always males. Small grouper eat crabs and small fishes, whereas large grouper probably eat large fishes.

Red-banded perch *Hypoplectrodes huntii* **Plate 43**

IDENTIFICATION: Body with *7 orange-brown bands* (first immediately behind head) *which reach down to belly,* tapering towards bottom; head orange-brown, often with greenish tinge on top; *fins red or orange.* Length 20 cm. Differs from half-banded perch (Plate 44) in number, colour and length of body bands, and in lacking a stripe through eye.

DISTRIBUTION: Three Kings Islands to Snares Islands; Chatham Islands. Endemic.

HABITAT: Rocky reefs with boulders, caves and overhangs.

GENERAL: Red-banded perch eat mainly crabs and small fishes, but also shellfish and brittlestars. Males grow larger than females. Other aspects of their biology are probably similar to those of half-banded perch.

Half-banded perch *Hypoplectrodes* sp.
Plate 44

IDENTIFICATION: Body with *6 blood-red bands which go halfway to two-thirds the way down flanks, and a red-brown band across nape which continues as stripe through eye and on to snout.* Head green-yellow above and white below; several yellow stripes on gill cover below eye. *Fins yellowish.* Length 15 cm. Differs from the red-banded perch (Plate 43) in number, colour and length of body bands, and in having stripe through eye.

DISTRIBUTION: Kermadec Islands; Three Kings Islands to East Cape. Most common around offshore islands and coastal headlands.

HABITAT: Reefs.

GENERAL: Half-banded perch spend much of the day resting under boulders or overhangs. At dusk they emerge to eat small crustaceans which they find among seaweed. They appear to begin life as females, and some of the population change sex to become males during the first year or two of life. Males grow larger than females and outnumber them in the population.

Males and females form stable pairs, occupying home ranges of about 2 square metres. Spawning occurs in spring and early summer, and small juveniles start appearing on the reefs in January–February. They grow rapidly, reaching maturity at 1 year old and a length of 6–9 cm. The oldest females are about 3 years, but males may live for 6 years.

Red-lined perch *Lepidoperca tasmanica*
Plate 35

IDENTIFICATION: Body white with *many wavy pink-red stripes,* arched on upper back; head pink-red above, white below; red spot on caudal peduncle. Length 20 cm.

DISTRIBUTION: Fiordland and Otago Peninsula to Snares Islands; Chatham Islands.

HABITAT: Steep walls, near boulders, crevices, overhangs and black coral trees. Usually deeper than 20 m.

GENERAL: Nothing is known of the biology of this species. Fiordland is the only place where it occurs within diving depths; elsewhere, it is found deeper than 150 m.

Toadstool grouper *Trachypoma macracanthus* **Plate 33**

IDENTIFICATION: *Orange, covered with numerous white dots.* Length 40 cm.

DISTRIBUTION: Kermadec Islands; Three Kings Islands to Aldermen Islands. Abundant at the Kermadecs, rare elsewhere. Most common around offshore islands and coastal headlands.

HABITAT: Under boulders, or in caves and crevices.

GENERAL: Toadstool grouper rest during the day, and can be approached closely. At night they roam in search of crustaceans, shellfish, and small fishes. Toadstool grouper are subtropical immigrants that arrive in northern New Zealand as larvae during warm summers.

CALLANTHIIDAE: Goldies

Small to medium, planktivorous, schooling fishes. Two species occur in New Zealand.

Southern splendid perch *Callanthias allporti*
Plate 42

IDENTIFICATION: *Pink body with yellowish head, chin and throat.* Upper and lower tail lobes usually yellowish; lobes in some individuals (perhaps the males) prolonged into filaments several centimetres long. Eye iridescent blue. Length 26 cm. Differs from northern splendid perch (Plates 40 and 41) in having only one colour phase, and in having a yellow chin and throat.

DISTRIBUTION: Kaikoura and Westport to Snares Islands; Chatham Islands.

HABITAT: Reefs, usually deeper than 25 m, but shallower in Fiordland.

GENERAL: Southern splendid perch behave similarly to their northern relative — they school with butterfly perch by day, presumably feeding on plankton, and retreat to caves and crevices in the reef when disturbed and at night.

Northern splendid perch *Callanthias australis* **Plates 40 and 41**

IDENTIFICATION: *Females uniformly pink-red. Males have deep mauve head and front of body, red rear body, yellow caudal peduncle and tail centre, and purple tail edges.* Male's anal and dorsal fins yellow or brown with blue margins. During spawning, males are orange-red, covered in white lattice pattern; white fins with red or orange markings, and red tips on tail. Length 30 cm. Differs from southern splendid perch (Plate 42) in having a distinctive male colour phase, and in lacking a yellow chin and throat.

DISTRIBUTION: Kermadec Islands; Three Kings Islands to Castlepoint and Westport.

HABITAT: Reefs, usually deeper than 25 m. Mainly around offshore islands and coastal headlands.

GENERAL: Northern splendid perch are usually seen near the bottom, frequently near a reef-sand boundary. They often school with pink maomao and butterfly perch, and are easily overlooked by divers. They eat plankton, especially crustaceans, and retreat to a cave or crevice in the reef when disturbed and at night.

Females are smaller than males, rarely exceeding 20 cm. School spawning has been observed in October: several males with their dorsal and anal fins raised spiral around one or two females; the group then swims upwards for several metres, releasing eggs and sperm at the peak of their movement.

FAMILY POLYPRIONIDAE:
Wreckfishes

Large, carnivorous, demersal fishes. Two species, hapuku and bass, occur in New Zealand. Bass *(Polyprion americanus)* occur in deeper water than hapuku and are rarely seen by divers.

Hapuku (Groper, Hāpuku) *Polyprion oxygeneios* **Plate 46**

IDENTIFICATION: *Blue-grey above, light grey to white below.* Head pointed and *lower jaw protrudes well beyond upper jaw.* Length 160 cm.

DISTRIBUTION: Three Kings Islands to Snares Islands; Chatham Islands; Campbell Islands.

HABITAT: Rugged, rocky areas such as pinnacles, caves and archways. Before they were heavily fished, hapuku were found from near the surface to deeper than 400 m. Now they are rarely seen shallower than 40 m, and then only at remote places.

GENERAL: Hapuku are gregarious, and when they were abundant in earlier years large schools were reported by divers. They make spawning migrations in July–September in central New Zealand, but the location of the spawning grounds, and details of the migrations, are unknown. Nowadays, divers are lucky to see one or two at a time. Hapuku are very curious, but wary.

Juvenile hapuku up to about 45 cm long are pelagic, and may associate with drifting seaweed, logs or floats; they are rarely seen. Hapuku are probably slow-growing and long-lived. Both sexes mature at about 85–90 cm. They eat a variety of fishes, squid and large crustaceans, including crayfish.

FAMILY CARANGIDAE: Jacks

Medium to large, planktivorous or carnivorous, pelagic species. Four species are common in coastal waters.

Koheru (Kōheru) *Decapterus koheru* **Plate 47**

IDENTIFICATION: *Blue-green above, with golden stripe along back;* silver below; tail yellow; small black spot on gill cover. *Pectoral fin short* (does not reach second dorsal fin). *Lateral line dips gently downwards* below second dorsal fin. Length 50 cm. Differs from jack mackerel (Plate 48) in length of pectoral fin, shape of lateral line and in lacking large ridged scales along lateral line.

DISTRIBUTION: Three Kings Islands to Cook Strait. Most abundant in the northern North Island. Endemic.

HABITAT: Forms midwater schools near reefs.

GENERAL: Koheru aggregate in large coordinated schools of fish of a similar size. They also associate with other larger fishes. Koheru feed indiscriminately on many types of plankton.

Koheru spawn in groups during the summer. Juveniles grow rapidly, reaching 20 cm after 1 year and about 30 cm after 2 years, and may live up to 10 years.

Trevally (Araara) *Pseudocaranx dentex* **Plate 49**

IDENTIFICATION: *Oval, silver body* with long

curved pectoral fin; black spot on gill cover; yellow tail. Juveniles up to 15 cm have 7–9 light grey bands on body, and fish up to 30 cm often have a yellow stripe from mid-body to tail. Adults have a grey-green back, and old fish may develop a humped head. Length 80 cm.

DISTRIBUTION: Kermadec Islands; Three Kings Islands to Stewart Island; Chatham Islands. Most abundant in the northern North Island, uncommon south of Cook Strait.

HABITAT: Juveniles occur in small groups in bays, harbours or near reefs, whereas adults form large schools near reefs or in open water.

GENERAL: Juvenile trevally less than 10 cm long are often seen riding the slipstream of other larger fishes. They also school with small jack mackerel, sweep and blue maomao. Juveniles eat small plankton, and also clean parasites from larger fishes. They frequently side-swipe the sand, possibly to remove their own parasites.

Adults form very large schools which range from the surface, where they eat planktonic crustaceans, to the bottom, where they eat crabs, brittlestars, heart urchins and bivalve shellfish. The adult schools are often associated with islands, pinnacles and headlands where plankton is concentrated by currents. At times, feeding trevally break the surface of the sea over a large area.

Trevally spawn during summer, with activity peaking in January–February. Juveniles grow to 10 cm after 1 year, and mature at 32–37 cm after 5 years, after which growth slows down. Trevally may live for 50 years.

Kingfish (Haku) *Seriola lalandi* **Plate 50**

IDENTIFICATION: *Long, streamlined body, green above* and white below; *green-gold stripe from snout through eye to yellow tail.* Length 160 cm.

DISTRIBUTION: Kermadec Islands; Three Kings Islands to Foveaux Strait; Chatham Islands. Uncommon south of Cook Strait, penetrating farthest south in summer and autumn.

HABITAT: Surface to seabed, from bays and harbours to reefs and open water.

GENERAL: Kingfish may occur singly or in schools of several hundred, often in association with other schooling species such as trevally and koheru. Kingfish schools are usually composed of similar-sized fish. They are attracted to divers, but usually remain for only a short time. Kingfish are voracious carnivores, eating a wide variety of small pelagic fishes such as koheru, blue maomao and trevally, and also small reef fishes which stray too far from shelter. They usually cruise slowly, but are capable of great acceleration when pursuing prey.

Kingfish spawn in summer, and small juveniles are pelagic, sheltering under drifting seaweed, logs and floats. They initially grow quickly, reaching 50 cm in 1–2 years, but their growth rate then slows down considerably.

Jack mackerel (Yellowtail, Hauture)
Trachurus novaezelandiae **Plate 48**

IDENTIFICATION: *Yellow-green with faint brown or grey bands above,* silver or white below; yellow tail; black spot on gill cover. Juveniles mostly silver. *A row of large, ridged scales along lateral line drops sharply* below second dorsal fin. *Pectoral fin long,* reaching beyond front of second dorsal fin. Length 55 cm. Differs from koheru (Plate 47) in length of pectoral fin, shape of lateral line, and size of lateral line scales. Two closely related species, *Trachurus declivis* and *T. murphyi* are difficult to

distinguish, but they tend to occur further offshore and are rarely seen by divers.

DISTRIBUTION: Cape Reinga to Foveaux Strait; Chatham Islands.

HABITAT: Forms schools in midwater, and ranges from shallow bays and harbours to oceanic islands and reefs.

GENERAL: Jack mackerel eat plankton and small pelagic fishes. They spawn in groups during spring–summer, and schools of mirror-like juveniles are seen close to reefs during autumn. They grow to 25 cm in 3 years, and may live to 28 years.

FAMILY ARRIPIDAE: Kahawai

Medium to large, planktivorous and carnivorous, schooling fishes. One species is common in New Zealand. Another species (*Arripis xylabion*) is common at the Kermadec Islands, and rare around the northern North Island.

Kahawai *Arripis trutta* **Plate 51**

IDENTIFICATION: *Blue-green above, silver below.* Adults have numerous black spots on back; juveniles have narrow black bands and black dots on back, and yellow-brown spots on sides. Length 60 cm.

DISTRIBUTION: Kermadec Islands; Three Kings Islands to Foveaux Strait; Chatham Islands.

HABITAT: Ranges from estuaries, bays and harbours to reefs and open water. Also penetrates rivers.

GENERAL: Kahawai form schools of similar-sized fish. Juveniles occur mostly in estuaries and shallow coastal waters, where they eat small plankton. Adults may occur singly or in huge schools which range from the surface to the seabed. When feeding at the surface, their backs and tails break the surface, causing characteristic disturbance patterns. Adults mainly eat large planktonic crustaceans and small schooling fishes (anchovies, pilchards, yellow-eyed mullet), but also eat crabs, worms and shellfish when feeding at the bottom. Kahawai are usually shy when seen underwater, and tend to move rapidly at the limit of a diver's visibility.

Kahawai spawn in January–March in the north, and March–April in the south. Juveniles reach 15 cm at the end of their first year, and mature at 35–40 cm after 4 or 5 years. They may live for 26 years.

FAMILY SPARIDAE: Breams and porgies

Medium to large, carnivorous, mainly demersal fishes. Most species undergo sex change at some stage in their lives. One species occurs in New Zealand.

Snapper (Tāmure) *Pagrus auratus* **Plate 53**

IDENTIFICATION: *Light copper-pink above,* fading to silver below; upper body covered in *numerous electric blue dots* (may fade in large fish); iridescent blue arc above eye (not visible from all angles); lower lobe of tail white. Juveniles have 4 or 5 dark bands on body, some of which split near the top. Length 105 cm.

DISTRIBUTION: Three Kings Islands to Foveaux Strait; Chatham Islands. Most abundant north of Cook Strait.

HABITAT: Ranges from estuaries and harbours to reefs and open bottom.

GENERAL: In most places, snapper are shy and flighty, and are usually seen near the limit of visibility. However, in some marine reserves they have been fed by divers and are attracted to a diver's noises. Snapper eat virtually any animal matter, which probably explains their wide habitat range and abundance. Diet changes considerably with size. Juveniles eat mainly small crustaceans which they find in or just above the sand, mud or coralline turf. As they grow, snapper eat a wider range of invertebrates, including crabs, worms and shellfish. Large snapper have powerful teeth, and can easily cope with hard-shelled animals such as paua, mussels, limpets and sea urchins. They also eat small fishes. At night, snapper rest upright in hollows in the seabed; the dark bands of the juveniles become more prominent, but the adults hardly change colour.

Adult snapper make seasonal inshore-offshore migrations, probably associated with spawning. Tagged adult snapper mostly moved less than 50 km from their tagging site, but a few moved several hundred kilometres. Very large, old snapper may stay on shallow reefs year-round.

Snapper spawn from September to March, with activity peaking in November–December. During summer they form large spawning aggregations in open water. Spawning occurs when several males and a female make upwards rushes of several metres before releasing clouds of eggs and sperm into the sea. Spawning takes place in the late afternoon or evening, and each fish probably spawns daily over an extended period. Fertilised eggs develop into larvae which drift in the plankton for 18–32 days. Juveniles then begin settling down to the bottom at a length of 2–3 cm during summer. They grow fastest during summer and autumn, and average 11–14 cm at the end of their first year.

All snapper begin life as females. During their third and fourth years about half of them change sex, going through a hermaphroditic stage, to become males.

By the time they mature, at about 23–26 cm and 3–5 years old, the population consists of about half males and half females. Snapper are long-lived, the oldest reaching 60 years.

FAMILY MULLIDAE: Goatfishes

Small to medium, carnivorous, demersal fishes with a pair of sensory barbels under the chin. Three species occur in New Zealand.

Black-spot goatfish *Parupeneus spilurus* **Plate 55**

IDENTIFICATION: Cream-white with *4 red-brown stripes* (bottom one quite pale) from snout to tail; *black spot near top of caudal peduncle.* Length 45 cm.

DISTRIBUTION: Kermadec Islands; Cape Reinga to East Cape. Common at the Kermadecs but rare in New Zealand.

HABITAT: Sandy areas near reefs.

GENERAL: Black-spot goatfish spend much of the day resting in the open or under ledges. They become active during the afternoon, when they forage for food in groups. They occur sporadically in New Zealand, suggesting that they are subtropical immigrants that arrive in northern New Zealand as larvae during warm summers.

Goatfish (Red mullet, Ahuruhuru) *Upeneichthys lineatus* **Plate 56**

IDENTIFICATION: Highly variable in colour, which can change dramatically in a few seconds. Most have a *dark brown or red broken stripe from eye to caudal peduncle, orange and blue wavy lines on head, and several rows of bright blue dots along body.* Blue dots or streaks on dorsal, anal and tail fins; *2 yellow barbels under chin.* Pale fish usually light yellow-brown above dark stripe, and white below; dark fish have *4 broad, brown to red bands on sides.* Large males have bright pink, mauve or red head, red belly, and yellow margins on dorsal fins. Amount of red on body varies from almost none to an almost complete cover. Length 40 cm.

DISTRIBUTION: Kermadec Islands; Three Kings Islands to Foveaux Strait. Rare south of Cook Strait.

HABITAT: Sand areas near reefs, or on sediment-covered reefs; occasionally seen in kelp forests.

GENERAL: Goatfish are highly variable in colour. Small goatfish and those feeding over sand tend to be pale, whereas those resting on the bottom on a reef are often almost scarlet. At night goatfish are usually bright red, but they may also be blotched with pink and white; the saddle pattern on the back is present but the spots fade.

Goatfish eat small invertebrates which they find by using their sensitive barbels. The barbels are very flexible and are flicked over and into the sand or coralline turf in front of the fish. Shellfish, worms and crustaceans are snapped up, and ingested sand is expelled through the gills. Juveniles spend much of their time feeding, but adults are often seen stacked in rows on the bottom, or resting in crevices or in the shelter of large sponges.

Spawning occurs in October–January. A pair moves upwards several metres and releases eggs and sperm before dropping back to the bottom. Juveniles 3–4 cm long appear near reef edges in January–April. They grow quickly, reaching about 15 cm after 1 year. Juvenile goatfish are very mobile, and usually have all fins raised. Females mature at the end of their first year, and males during their second year.

Bar-tailed goatfish *Upeneus francisi* **Plate 54**

IDENTIFICATION: *White or silver with 4 rows of brown spots on back; tail with 4 pairs of orange and white bars on upper lobe, orange stripe on lower lobe;* 2 white barbels under chin. Length 15 cm.

DISTRIBUTION: Kermadec Islands; Cape Reinga to Leigh. Rare.

HABITAT: Sand bottom adjacent to reefs.

GENERAL: Bar-tailed goatfish swim in small schools close to the bottom. Their light colour provides excellent camouflage over sand. They move constantly, probing the sand with their barbels, and sometimes the whole head, for small crustaceans and worms. At night, bar-tailed goatfish rest near the bottom and change colour to white with red and brown spots and blotches.

Bar-tailed goatfish are subtropical immigrants that arrive in northern New Zealand as larvae during warm summers. Because of their small size, cryptic coloration and sand habitat, they are probably often overlooked.

FAMILY PEMPHERIDAE: Bullseyes

Small, planktivorous, demersal and midwater fishes. One species is common in New Zealand.

Bigeye *Pempheris adspersus* **Plate 22**

IDENTIFICATION: *Body deep, tapering sharply upwards towards tail;* eye large. *Copper or brown* with black tips on dorsal and anal fins. Length 17 cm.

DISTRIBUTION: Three Kings Islands to East Cape. Endemic.

HABITAT: Reefs, in caves or under overhangs.

GENERAL: Bigeyes are nocturnal, hiding in caves during the day and emerging at dusk to feed on large plankton. Their large eyes enable them to see their prey even in dim light. They spawn during summer, and juveniles 1–2 cm long are seen in January–March hiding among kelp, where they are well camouflaged by their golden yellow colour. Juveniles feed during the day on small plankton.

FAMILY KYPHOSIDAE: Drummers

Medium to large, planktivorous or herbivorous reef fishes. Two species occur in New Zealand, and they are most abundant around the northern half of the North Island.

Grey drummer *Kyphosus bigibbus* **Plate 57**

IDENTIFICATION: *Olive green, grey or brown above, silver or grey below; silver streak below eye.* Fins pale or dusky. Juveniles have large pale spots on body. A rare colour form is bright yellow with white belly and black eyes. Length 40 cm. Differs from silver drummer (Plate 58) in having a more slender body, paler fins and smaller size.

DISTRIBUTION: Kermadec Islands; Cape Reinga to Poor Knights Islands.

HABITAT: Surgy shallow water near reefs.

GENERAL: Grey drummer school near the surface or sometimes in midwater. They eat fine turfing seaweeds, grazing them from the rocks in rapid, coordinated feeding bouts. They also eat plankton. Grey drummer are less common than silver drummer around mainland New Zealand, but their true abundance is unknown because the two species have previously been confused.

Silver drummer *Kyphosus sydneyanus* **Plate 58**

IDENTIFICATION: *Heavy-bodied with broad, black-edged tail. Body grey to olive green above, silver below,* sometimes with grey or green stripes along belly; head has silver and grey markings; all fins black. Juveniles olive green, sometimes with rows of white spots on body. Length 70 cm. Differs from grey drummer (Plate 57) in having a deeper, thicker body, black fins and greater size.

DISTRIBUTION: Three Kings Islands to Cook Strait. Most abundant in the north.

HABITAT: Turbulent, shallow water (less than 10 m) near reefs.

GENERAL: Silver drummer are usually seen in fast-moving schools. They are wary and difficult to approach, but are also inquisitive and may make a number of fast runs past a diver. They are herbivorous, eating large brown seaweed, fine red and green seaweed, and a variety of invertebrates (which may be taken incidentally). Drummer feed mainly at dawn and dusk. Juveniles appear in very shallow, surgy water during January–April. They are more cryptic in colour and behaviour than the adults and are rarely seen.

FAMILY GIRELLIDAE: Nibblers

Medium to large, omnivorous fishes. Two species occur in northern New Zealand.

Bluefish (Korokoropounamu) *Girella cyanea* **Plate 59**

IDENTIFICATION: *Light or bright blue,* but can appear dark grey in dim light; body covered with *gold spots.* Length 65 cm.

DISTRIBUTION: Kermadec Islands; Three Kings Islands to Cook Strait. Most common around the northern offshore islands and at the Kermadecs.

HABITAT: Shallow reefs with caves, tunnels and large boulders, usually shallower than 10 m.

GENERAL: Bluefish use their 3-pointed teeth to browse small invertebrates (crustaceans, brittlestars, tube worms) and seaweed from the rocks. They feed mainly at dawn and dusk, and are wary and difficult to approach during the day. They are probably summer spawners.

Parore *Girella tricuspidata* **Plate 60**

IDENTIFICATION: *Silver-grey with 9–12 fine, black bands;* lips and face have golden tinge. Length 45 cm.

DISTRIBUTION: Three Kings Islands to Cook Strait. Most abundant in the north.

HABITAT: Ranges from mangrove forests and estuaries to reefs. Usually in less than 10 m of water.

GENERAL: Parore are usually seen in schools, but they are very shy and are often seen fleetingly. The diet varies with growth. Small juveniles eat plankton, detritus, and parasites that they clean from other fishes. Larger juveniles eat increasing amounts of filamentous seaweed and detritus. Adults are mainly herbivorous, eating a mixture of fine filamentous seaweed, large brown seaweed, and invertebrates. The teeth are used in a shearing action to remove slices of seaweed, which are then swallowed whole. They feed throughout the day. At night parore shelter under boulders and in crevices; the body darkens, the bands become indistinct, and the head and upper back become blotched with light grey or cream.

Parore spawn during spring–summer, and juveniles 2 cm long settle in estuaries and bays during late summer. They grow to 10 cm by the end of their first year, and 15 cm by the end of their second. Parore mature at about 28 cm and 5 years old, and may live for 10 years.

FAMILY SCORPIDAE: Stonebreams

Small to medium, planktivorous fishes. Four species occur in northern New Zealand.

Grey knifefish *Bathystethus cultratus* **Plate 61**

IDENTIFICATION: Small head and *deep, rounded belly profile. Back blue-green to grey; sides and belly silver.* Length 30 cm.

DISTRIBUTION: Kermadec Islands; Three Kings Islands to Mayor Island. Mainly around offshore islands and coastal headlands.

HABITAT: Areas of white surgy water around islands and points. Usually shallower than 15 m.

GENERAL: Grey knifefish occur in small schools, and are wary and difficult to approach. They eat small plankton. Grey knifefish are subtropical immigrants that arrive in northern New Zealand as larvae during warm summers.

Blue knifefish *Labracoglossa nitida* **Plate 62**

IDENTIFICATION: *Bright blue with yellow streak on back and caudal peduncle, fading on head and tail; black spot at base of pectoral fin.* Length 25 cm.

DISTRIBUTION: Kermadec Islands; Cape Reinga to East Cape. Common at the Kermadecs, uncommon in New Zealand. Mainly around offshore islands.

HABITAT: Open water near islands, pinnacles and headlands. Usually shallower than 20 m.

GENERAL: Blue knifefish form small, fast-moving schools. They eat large planktonic crustaceans. Blue knifefish are subtropical immigrants that arrive in northern New Zealand as larvae during warm summers. In some years they are common at offshore islands and around coastal headlands.

Sweep (Hui) *Scorpis lineolatus* **Plate 63**

IDENTIFICATION: *Blue-grey with oval to diamond-shaped body and small head.* Juveniles up to 8 cm grey-green with orange spots on body. Length 35 cm. Differs from blue maomao (Plate 64) in colour; sweep lack yellow anal fins as juveniles.

DISTRIBUTION: Three Kings Islands to Fiordland. Most abundant in the north; rare south of Cook Strait.

HABITAT: Juveniles are found on shallow reefs, close to shelter. Adults may school in midwater, and range from shallow turbulent waters to deep reefs.

GENERAL: Sweep eat small plankton, which they catch individually with a snapping movement of the lower jaw. They spawn in winter, and the juveniles are found hiding in reef crevices from July to October. They reach 15–20 cm at the end of their first year.

Blue maomao (Maomao) *Scorpis violaceus* **Plate 64**

IDENTIFICATION: *Iridescent blue. Usually seen in schools* of a dozen to thousands. Juveniles blue but lack iridescence of adults; anal fin yellow until they reach 17–19 cm. Length 40 cm. Differs from sweep (Plate 63) in colour.

DISTRIBUTION: Kermadec Islands; Three Kings Islands to Kaikoura. Most abundant at the Kermadecs and around northeastern North Island.

HABITAT: Similar to sweep; large schools of adults occur near archways and headlands, particularly around offshore islands.

GENERAL: Blue maomao feed midwater or at the surface on planktonic crustaceans, salps, fish eggs and larvae, and seaweed (which is possibly ingested incidentally). Large schools are frequently seen breaking the surface as the fish surge forward, catching their prey with snapping movements of the lower jaw. At night, adults swim slowly near the bottom, remaining alert.

Blue maomao actively solicit the services of cleanerfish, and frequently rub their flanks on the bottom, possibly to dislodge skin parasites. Spawning occurs in winter. Juveniles settle onto the reefs in October–January, and for the first year they remain close to the bottom. Blue maomao grow to 10 cm by the end of their first year, and 24 cm at 5 years old.

FAMILY MICROCANTHIDAE: Mados

Small to medium, carnivorous fishes. One species occurs in New Zealand.

Mado *Atypichthys latus* **Plate 52**

IDENTIFICATION: White with *5 or 6 dark brown stripes,* some of which continue obliquely down snout; *fins yellow.* Length 30 cm.

DISTRIBUTION: Kermadec Islands; Three Kings Islands to East Cape. Most common around offshore islands.

HABITAT: Reefs, especially near caves, archways and overhangs.

GENERAL: Mado usually swim alone or in small groups, but can form large schools. They eat crustaceans, worms, anemones, hydroids and seaweed grazed from rock walls or boulders. Juveniles may act as cleaners, picking crustacean parasites off larger fishes. They probably spawn in winter.

FAMILY CHAETODONTIDAE: Butterflyfishes

Small to medium, carnivorous, demersal fishes. One species occurs in New Zealand.

Lord Howe coralfish *Amphichaetodon howensis* **Plate 65**

IDENTIFICATION: *Head silver, body yellow with 5 black bands,* the first passing through eye and the last across caudal peduncle; narrow black stripe along snout. Length 25 cm.

DISTRIBUTION: Kermadec Islands; Three Kings Islands to Mahia Peninsula. Most common around offshore islands and coastal headlands.

HABITAT: Reefs, near caves, archways and overhangs. Usually deeper than 20 m.

GENERAL: Lord Howe coralfish are usually seen in pairs, and probably mate for life. They are home-ranging, and are frequently seen in the same locality. They eat a variety of invertebrates, especially crustaceans, which they extract from among sponges, bryozoans and ascidians using their long snouts and small jaws.

FAMILY PENTACEROTIDAE: Boarfishes

Medium to large, carnivorous, demersal fishes with large bony heads. Body and dorsal fin shapes usually change with age; in particular, the snout may elongate greatly. Three species occur in coastal waters.

Striped boarfish *Evistias acutirostris* **Plate 66**

IDENTIFICATION: Oval body with protruding snout and sail-like dorsal fin. *White with 5 black bands on body;* face and snout black; *fins yellow,* except for the black pelvic fins. Length 60 cm.

DISTRIBUTION: Kermadec Islands; Cape Reinga to Mayor Island. Occasional at the Kermadecs, rare in New Zealand.

HABITAT: Reefs, usually in caves or archways, but may occur in the open.

GENERAL: Striped boarfish probably eat invertebrates, like other members of the family. They are usually in pairs or small groups, but an aggregation of 43 has been seen at the Kermadecs.

Giant boarfish *Paristiopterus labiosus*
Plate 67

IDENTIFICATION: Body elongated, especially snout. *Silver-grey with 2 oblique, irregularly shaped, green-brown patches;* irregular stripe along belly. *Some individuals, possibly spawning males, covered in dense yellow dots. Juveniles deeper-bodied,* with shorter snouts than adults. Their colour pattern is similar to that of adults, but the oblique patches and stripe are darker and more distinct. Length 85 cm.

DISTRIBUTION: Three Kings Islands to Foveaux Strait.

HABITAT: Open sand or mud bottom, occasionally seen near reef edges.

GENERAL: Giant boarfish feed over sand and mud, using their elongated snouts to probe for crabs, bivalves, worms, brittlestars and sea cucumbers. Occasionally seen by divers when the fish move close to reefs, and may remain in one place for several weeks. Yellow-spotted individuals (Plate 67) are seen mainly in summer and are thought to be courting males. However, they have also been seen in winter.

Long-finned boarfish *Zanclistius elevatus*
Plate 68

IDENTIFICATION: *Very tall, sail-like dorsal fin with black blotch near rear edge.* Silver-grey with *2 large, oblique, irregular brown patches on side;* light brown band from nape through eye. Length 35 cm.

DISTRIBUTION: Cape Reinga to Cook Strait. Most common in the north.

HABITAT: Reefs deeper than 25 m; also over open bottom.

GENERAL: Long-finned boarfish are home-ranging, occurring in the same place for several years. They are usually solitary, but aggregations of up to 20 fish have been seen. They eat crabs, worms and brittlestars, which they pry out of crevices with their pointed snouts.

FAMILY POMACENTRIDAE:
Damselfishes

Small to medium, mainly planktivorous or herbivorous reef fishes. Many species lay eggs in nests on the bottom, where they are guarded by the males until they hatch. Six species have been reported from coastal waters, though one is very rare.

Demoiselle *Chromis dispilus* **Plates 69 and 70**

IDENTIFICATION: *Adults blue-grey with 2 white spots on back* and a black blotch at base of pectoral fin. Spawning males bright blue, with white tail fork and rear edge of dorsal and anal fins. *Juveniles olive green with 2 white spots.* Length 18 cm.

DISTRIBUTION: Kermadec Islands; Three Kings Islands to Mahia Peninsula and Cape Egmont. Endemic.

HABITAT: Adults school in midwater near cliff faces, pinnacles and archways, except during the spawning season when males are found near the bottom. Juveniles stay close to the reef for shelter.

GENERAL: Demoiselles eat small planktonic crustaceans, fish eggs and larvae, and other plankton. They congregate in areas where currents bring them a steady supply of food. Demoiselles use their pectoral fins for maintaining position facing into the current, and snap up their prey as it drifts past. At night they rest on the bottom, in crevices or in the open; their colour becomes blotchy and the white spots fade.

During the November–March spawning season females lay their eggs on rock surfaces, where the males guard them against predators. Peak spawning activity occurs in December–January, and is synchronous.

Large numbers of demoiselles spawn in the same place at the same time, and all the eggs hatch out within a few days. Males select the nest sites, which may be as little as 10 cm apart. Females hover in groups above the nest sites, and each male makes upward forays to try to entice a female down to lay eggs. She attaches her sticky eggs to the rock as she makes a number of close passes over the nest site. The male swims in the opposite direction, fertilising the eggs as they are released. The nest is built up over several days, and may reach 30 cm in diameter.

Both sexes are promiscuous, with females laying eggs in several different nests, and males attracting several different females to their nests. The eggs are visible as small clear or pink spheres packed closely together in a mat. The male aggressively defends his nest against predators such as wrasses and triplefins, and drives off fishes many times his size. The eggs hatch at night about a week after being laid, and the young larvae move up into the plankton.

Juveniles 1–2 cm long settle back on to the reef a month later, and hide in caves and crevices in small groups. They grow rapidly, reaching 10 cm in 4 months, and move progressively out into open water where they form schools.

Yellow demoiselle *Chromis fumea* **Plate 71**

IDENTIFICATION: *Yellow above, silver below;*

white dot on caudal peduncle; *tail brown- or black-striped along top and bottom margins.* Length 10 cm.

DISTRIBUTION: Cape Reinga to Poor Knights Islands. Rare. Usually seen around offshore islands and coastal headlands.

HABITAT: Reefs.

GENERAL: Yellow demoiselles eat plankton, but do not school in midwater like the other two demoiselle species. They aggregate in groups of up to 25 fish close to the reef. They appear intermittently in New Zealand, suggesting they do not breed here, but drift down as larvae from subtropical waters.

Single-spot demoiselle *Chromis hypsilepis* **Plate 72**

IDENTIFICATION: *Body yellow-green;* head yellow, particularly just behind eye; *white spot on top of caudal peduncle,* and black spot at base of pectoral fin. Length 18 cm.

DISTRIBUTION: Three Kings Islands to Mayor Island. Most common around offshore islands and coastal headlands.

HABITAT: Midwater, near reefs.

GENERAL: Single-spot demoiselles generally school with ordinary demoiselles, and eat small planktonic crustaceans. They spawn in February, at least, and possibly throughout the summer. Females lay eggs on rock faces where they are fertilised and guarded by the males.

Black angelfish *Parma alboscapularis* **Plates 73 and 74**

IDENTIFICATION: *Adults black, often with white blotch above upper corner of gill cover;* teeth, eyes and parts of face white. *Juveniles up to about 15 cm long yellow-brown with numerous electric blue dots, some arranged in rows; black spot on upper back* and blue margins on dorsal, anal and pelvic fins. Length 30 cm.

DISTRIBUTION: Kermadec Islands; Three Kings Islands to Castlepoint and Albatross Point. Most common around offshore islands and coastal headlands.

HABITAT: Reefs, near boulders and caves. Usually less than 10 m deep.

GENERAL: Black angelfish are herbivorous, selectively browsing fine red and green seaweed in shallow water. Their teeth, which are arranged into two cutting plates, are used like shears. Males defend territories in open, bouldery areas devoid of large brown seaweed. Each territory has rock faces for nest sites, and caves or crevices for shelter. During the November–January breeding season, less so at other times, males aggressively confront each other at their territory boundaries. They flash their white shoulder patches and raise their fins to assert their dominance. The loser in these border disputes flees in submission, his white patch fading to grey in a few seconds.

Each male cultivates a nest site on a slightly overhanging face of a boulder. He removes any small animals from the site, and nips off the tops of seaweed, leaving a short turf of fine red and green seaweed. Invertebrates that move into the nest site, or settle out of the plankton onto it, are removed. The nest sites are maintained year-round, and are easily recognisable outside the spawning season. Females lay their sticky eggs on the seaweed as they make spawning passes across the turf, and the male fertilises them while swimming in the opposite direction. Several batches of eggs are laid in the nest over a few days, until a circular or oval nest up to 80 cm in diameter is formed. Each nest may contain eggs from several females. The male guards his nest aggressively against predators, attacking and chasing off fishes several times his size. The eggs hatch into planktonic larvae after about 7–10 days. Juveniles 2–5 cm long are first seen hiding under boulders and in crevices in less than 5 m of water during summer. They grow rapidly, reaching adult size after about 18 months.

FAMILY CHIRONEMIDAE: Kelpfishes

Small to medium, carnivorous, demersal fishes. One species occurs in New Zealand.

Hiwihiwi (Kelpfish) *Chironemus marmoratus* **Plate 75**

IDENTIFICATION: *Mosaic of light (fawn or pink) and dark (brown, red-brown or olive-green) patches, overlaid with dense white dots.* Length 35 cm.

DISTRIBUTION: Cape Reinga to Cook Strait. Most abundant in the north.

HABITAT: Reefs, near or in caves and crevices. Usually shallower than 25 m.

GENERAL: Hiwihiwi are usually seen propped up on their pectoral, pelvic and anal fins. This pose provides good stability and grip on the rocks, and enables hiwihiwi to inhabit shallow, surgy water. They occur in small groups, which have home ranges centred on caves or crevices, in which they spend much of the day. They are also often seen in the open, darting back to shelter if disturbed.

Hiwihiwi appear to make seasonal movements between very shallow water in summer and deeper (15–25 m) water in winter. These movements may be associated with spawning, which occurs in winter. Fish less than 10 cm long are always found in shallow water, often in very surgy places.

Hiwihiwi feed mainly at dawn and dusk, and eat a wide range of invertebrates (especially crabs, limpets and chitons) and small triplefins. Hiwihiwi are very curious, but are also easily frightened.

FAMILY APLODACTYLIDAE:
Marblefishes

Medium to large, herbivorous, demersal fishes. Two species occur in New Zealand.

Marblefish (Kehe) *Aplodactylus arctidens* Plate 76

IDENTIFICATION: *Olive green or brown, heavily marbled with white* except on some parts of back. *Swimming motion very sinuous.* Length 70 cm. Differs from notch-head marblefish (Plate 77) in colour and head profile.

DISTRIBUTION: Three Kings Islands to Snares Islands; Chatham Islands.

HABITAT: Reefs, near caves and crevices. Usually shallower than 15 m.

GENERAL: Marblefish swim with an exaggerated, sinuous motion, and with pectoral and dorsal fins raised. They often swim straight towards a diver, stop a metre away, then dash away again. They may make two or three such approaches before disappearing into a hole. Marblefish are solitary and home-ranging. They are most active at dawn and dusk, and usually rest in caves and crevices during the day and night. They graze mainly on red and small brown seaweed with their downward-pointing mouths and slicing teeth. Marblefish spawn in August–September.

Notch-head marblefish *Aplodactylus etheridgii* Plate 77

IDENTIFICATION: *Olive-brown, covered in dense white dots;* row of white spots underneath dorsal fins; *2 or 3 larger white blotches along middle of body; gill membranes orange. Head profile has 'notch' behind eyes.* Length 45 cm. Differs from marblefish (Plate 76) in colour and head profile.

DISTRIBUTION: Kermadec Islands; Three Kings Islands to Great Barrier Island. Abundant at the Kermadecs, uncommon in New Zealand where it occurs mainly around offshore islands and coastal headlands.

HABITAT: Reefs. Usually shallower than 15 m.

GENERAL: Probably similar to common marblefish in biology and behaviour.

FAMILY CHEILODACTYLIDAE:
Morwongs

Medium to large, carnivorous, demersal fishes. Morwongs have thick fleshy lips which they seal around the substrate when they are feeding. Small invertebrates and sediment are sucked into the mouth, and sand and mud are ejected out of the gills before the food is crushed and swallowed. Morwongs have one or more elongated pectoral fin rays; these extend only slightly beyond the fin edge in red and painted moki, but are very long in tarakihi and porae. Six species occur in New Zealand but two are rare.

Painted moki *Cheilodactylus ephippium* Plate 78

IDENTIFICATION: *Cream-white with 3 brown bands:* the first runs from nape behind gills; the second and third run obliquely across body (the third sometimes expands to cover rear of body). *Three white blotches on back;* red bases to pectoral, pelvic and anal fins, and rear edge of gill cover; brown or black line circles eye; *head and lower body dotted orange.* Length 55 cm.

41

DISTRIBUTION: Kermadec Islands; Three Kings Islands to Bay of Plenty. Abundant at the Kermadecs, rare in New Zealand where it occurs mainly around offshore islands and coastal headlands.

HABITAT: Reefs.

GENERAL: Painted moki are often seen in caves or crevices by day, but they also rove around the reef. Mainly solitary in New Zealand, but at the Kermadecs they occur in small groups. They eat small invertebrates.

Red moki (Nanua) *Cheilodactylus spectabilis* Plate 79

IDENTIFICATION: *White with 8 broad, red-brown bands* (including nape and tail bands) which taper towards belly; sometimes several bands fuse together, and some fish may be uniformly red-brown without obvious bands. Upper head brown; body above pectoral fin orange. Length 70 cm.

DISTRIBUTION: Three Kings Islands to Foveaux Strait; Chatham Islands. Most abundant in the north, rare south of Cook Strait.

HABITAT: Reefs, near caves, overhangs or crevices.

GENERAL: Red moki may be seen roving over the reef, through kelp forests, or huddled in caves during the day. At night they rest in caves, and their contrasting bands fade. Red moki feed mainly at dawn and dusk. They orientate themselves head-downwards, and 'bump' into the seabed, taking a mouthful of sediment and invertebrate food while the pectoral and tail fins beat to provide force and manoeuvrability. They mainly eat small crustaceans, crabs, brittlestars and sea urchins.

Red moki are home-ranging, occupying the same area for several years. Adult females occur in groups in water shallower than 15 m for most of the year, whereas males are solitary and inhabit deep reefs. Males are territorial, and appear to defend cave sites from each other. The size of their territories increases with the size of the male. In March–May females migrate to deeper water during the day and at dusk to spawn with the males; spawning possibly occurs in the caves occupied by the males. Juveniles 3–4 cm long appear in very shallow water (less than 5 m) or in rockpools during September–November after a planktonic larval life of several months. They are silvery with very distinct bands, and unlike the adults they spend much of the day feeding. They grow rapidly to reach about 15 cm after 6 months. Females mature at about 25 cm, males at 30 cm, after about 2 years. Growth then slows dramatically, and large fish may be up to 60 years old. Males grow bigger and faster than females.

Porae *Nemadactylus douglasii* Plate 80

IDENTIFICATION: *Blue-green to turquoise above, often with a golden sheen, and blue-grey below;* appear blue-grey in natural light. One very long pectoral fin ray. Length 70 cm.

DISTRIBUTION: Kermadec Islands; Three Kings Islands to Kaikoura. Rare at the Kermadecs, most abundant in the northern North Island.

HABITAT: Sand, or reefs with sand or gravel patches.

GENERAL: Porae are active during the day, feeding on small invertebrates which occur in sand, gravel and coralline turf. They eat a wide variety of animals, especially worms, brittlestars, small sea urchins and crustaceans. Porae are usually solitary, but large aggregations have been seen in deeper water. They are home-ranging, and may be seen in the same place for several years. At night porae remain alert and ready to flee, but can be approached closely.

Porae probably spawn during late summer and autumn, and larvae have a long planktonic life. They settle onto the bottom, probably over sand in deep water, at a length of about 10 cm in midsummer. They grow rapidly and reach 25–28 cm after 2 years, but growth then slows down markedly. Large fish may be more than 30 years old.

Tarakihi *Nemadactylus macropterus* Plate 81

IDENTIFICATION: *Grey or silver (darker above than below) with prominent black nape band.* One very long pectoral fin ray. Length 70 cm.

DISTRIBUTION: Three Kings Islands to Snares Islands; Chatham Islands.

HABITAT: Mud or sand, occasionally near reef edges.

GENERAL: Tarakihi occur singly or in small groups near reef edges, but over soft bottom they may form large schools. They are usually seen deeper than 25 m in northern New Zealand but may be shallower in the south. They feed mainly at dusk, on worms, crabs, brittlestars and shellfish which they suck from the sand or mud. At night tarakihi rest in depressions on the bottom, and their colour becomes blotchy.

Tarakihi spawn in large aggregations in only a few known regions — East Cape, the northeast coast of the South Island, and Fiordland. Tagging shows that some fish migrate over 500 km along the east coast of both North and South Islands, presumably for spawning. Tarakihi spawn in March–June near East Cape (activity peaking in April–May), but progressively earlier further south (January–February at Kaikoura). Tarakihi segregate by sex during the breeding season, and spawn during the night. Eggs are released in batches, and individual fish may spawn periodically over several months.

Tarakihi have a planktonic larval stage of 7–10 months, after which juveniles about 7–9 cm long settle to the bottom during early summer. Juveniles concentrate in areas of rough bottom, and nursery grounds occur in Manawatu, Tasman Bay, along the east coast of the South Island, and at the Chatham Islands. Juveniles eat small crustaceans, and remain in the nursery grounds until they mature after 4–5 years. Males mature at 25–30 cm and females at 28–34 cm. Females grow bigger and faster than males, and the oldest tarakihi may reach 45 years old.

FAMILY LATRIDAE: Trumpeters

Medium to large, carnivorous, demersal or pelagic fishes. Four species occur in New Zealand.

Blue moki (Moki) *Latridopsis ciliaris* Plate 82

IDENTIFICATION: *Blue-grey above, often with light and dark banding; silver below.* Lips large and fleshy. Length 90 cm. Differs from copper moki (Plate 83) in colour.

DISTRIBUTION: Kermadec Islands; Three Kings Islands to Snares Islands; Chatham Islands; Auckland Islands. Uncommon north of East Cape, rare at the Kermadecs. Juveniles less than about 30 cm have not been recorded north of East Cape.

HABITAT: Adults occur mainly over sand or mud bottom, but are occasionally seen over reefs. Juveniles less than 30 cm live mainly on reefs.

GENERAL: Adult blue moki eat crabs, other crustaceans, shellfish and worms which they suck from the sand or mud. They form large schools which make annual migrations along the east coast of New Zealand to the only known spawning ground near Gisborne. Moki from as far away as Kaikoura, Manawatu and Bay of Plenty converge on Gisborne in August to spawn, and the spent fish return along the same routes. Some tagged fish have migrated over 500 km. A small proportion of adults apparently do not join these migrations, and can be seen on or near reefs year-round. Eggs and larvae spawned off Gisborne are carried southwards by the East Cape Current, thus accounting for the lack of juveniles in the north. Juveniles settle onto shallow reefs at a length of about 10 cm, after a larval life of 8–12 months. They eat mainly small crustaceans which they find among seaweed. Maturity is reached at about 40 cm and 5–6 years, at which time moki move offshore to join the migratory adult schools. The oldest moki may live for over 30 years.

Copper moki *Latridopsis forsteri* **Plate 83**

IDENTIFICATION: *Silver-white with several copper-brown stripes on back;* pectoral fin copper-brown with black margin, and tail and second dorsal fin also have black margins. Length 65 cm. Differs from blue moki (Plate 82) in colour.

DISTRIBUTION: Cape Reinga to Stewart Island. Rare north of East Cape and Albatross Point.

HABITAT: As for blue moki.

GENERAL: Copper moki often occur in association with blue moki, but are much less abundant. They eat mainly crustaceans, but worms and small fishes increase in importance in larger fish. Growth rates and spawning behaviour are similar to those of blue moki. They mature at about 40 cm and 5 years, at which time they move out of shallow coastal waters. Copper moki are found in the blue moki spawning schools, suggesting that they also migrate along the east coast of New Zealand to spawn near Gisborne.

Trumpeter (Kohikohi) *Latris lineata* **Plate 84**

IDENTIFICATION: *White with 3 black stripes on back:* two continue down face, the third arcs around gill cover. A *broad black stripe along lower side fades towards tail; fins yellow; face and back may have yellowish tinge.* Length 110 cm.

DISTRIBUTION: Poor Knights Islands and Cape Egmont to Snares Islands; Chatham Islands; Auckland Islands. Rare north of Cook Strait.

HABITAT: Reefs.

GENERAL: Trumpeter are usually seen singly or in small groups over shallow reefs, but they may form large aggregations in deeper water. They frequently school with blue and copper moki. Trumpeter eat any large prey, including crabs, octopus, squid and small fishes. They have also been seen feeding on large swarms of planktonic crustaceans. Trumpeter spawn in winter.

Telescopefish (Koihi) *Mendosoma lineatum* **Plate 85**

IDENTIFICATION: *Blue-green above with many fine brown stripes; silver below.* Length 40 cm.

DISTRIBUTION: Kapiti Island and Castlepoint to Snares Islands; Chatham Islands; Auckland Islands. Most common in the south.

HABITAT: Forms fast-moving schools near reefs.

GENERAL: Telescopefish have protrusible,

'telescoping' jaws which they use to snap up planktonic crustaceans and small fishes. Juveniles are more silvery than adults, giving their schools a shimmering appearance. Telescopefish probably spawn year-round, but activity peaks from late winter to late summer.

FAMILY MUGILIDAE: Mullets

Small to medium, schooling fishes which eat plankton and organic matter in seabed sediments. One species is commonly seen in coastal waters.

Yellow-eyed mullet (Aua) *Aldrichetta forsteri* **Plate 147**

IDENTIFICATION: *Grey-green above, silver below; eye yellow.* Length 40 cm.

DISTRIBUTION: Cape Reinga to Stewart Island; Chatham Islands.

HABITAT: Estuaries, harbours and sheltered bays. Also penetrates rivers.

GENERAL: Yellow-eyed mullet form large schools in sheltered waters. They penetrate into estuaries and freshwater during summer. They are often incorrectly called 'sprats' and 'herrings'. Yellow-eyed mullet have two different feeding modes: they digest the organic matter and small invertebrates from large quantities of mud that they scoop up from the seabed; and they also eat planktonic crustaceans.

They spawn from late winter to summer, and juveniles are first found in estuaries during early summer. With the approach of winter they move out into coastal waters. Yellow-eyed mullet mature at about 3 years, at lengths of 14–15 cm for males and 17 cm for females. Females grow faster, and reach a greater size, than males.

FAMILY LABRIDAE: Wrasses

Small to medium, carnivorous, demersal fishes which swim with a sculling action of their pectoral fins, and use their tails only for rapid swimming. Wrasses pick invertebrates from seaweed or rocks with their large canine teeth. The juveniles of some species act as cleanerfish, removing parasites from the bodies of larger fishes.

Wrasses have complex social systems. Most fish develop first into females when they mature, and some eventually change sex to become males. Females generally outnumber males in the population. Males often defend territories against each other by aggressively confronting any intruders, and displaying their large, colourful dorsal and anal fins to increase their apparent size and visibility. When a male dies, a large female may change sex and take over his territory.

Spawning has been observed in many species of wrasse and appears to follow a common pattern. After courtship, which always involves a male displaying to a female with his dorsal and anal fins, both sexes swim rapidly towards the surface while almost touching. As the water pressure drops suddenly the swim bladder expands, placing pressure on the gonads and squeezing sperm and eggs out into the water. Both sexes then return to the bottom, often to repeat the spawning manoeuvres. Spawning may take place in pairs or in groups.

Wrasses have two or three distinct colour patterns associated with the different phases of development. Males and females are usually differently coloured (though a few males may exhibit the female colour pattern), and juveniles of some species are also distinctive. Intermediate stages are rarely seen because the transitions between colour phases are rapid. Males are usually deeper-bodied, and have blunter heads than females.

Sixteen species of wrasse have been recorded in New Zealand. However, a number of these only reach northern New Zealand from subtropical waters during warm summers. Some species are known here only as juveniles, which apparently do not survive the winter. Ten species appear to be permanent New Zealand residents, but some of these may not successfully spawn here, their populations being maintained by continual recruitment of larvae from subtropical areas.

Elegant wrasse *Anampses elegans* **Plates 86 and 87**

IDENTIFICATION: Two colour phases — female and male. Colour and sex changes occur at 20 cm. *Females yellow above,* silver below, *with rows of blue dots and vertical dashes; grey mask between eyes;* anal fin yellow and tail dusky yellow. *Males olive green above, abruptly pale below; covered with numerous vertical blue lines. Prominent blue lines through eye; orange and black blotches on rear of gill cover;* tail yellow. Length 30 cm.

DISTRIBUTION: Kermadec Islands; Cape Reinga to Poor Knights Islands.

HABITAT: Reefs in sheltered bays and harbours.

GENERAL: Juveniles and females aggregate in small, fast-moving groups that pause only to browse on the seabed for their food, which consists mainly of crustaceans and worms. Males are much less common than females, and are solitary. They occur down to about 30 m, whereas females and juveniles are seldom seen deeper than 10 m. Elegant wrasse are subtropical immigrants that arrive in northern New Zealand as larvae during warm summers.

Red pigfish (Pākurakura) *Bodianus unimaculatus* **Plates 88 and 89**

IDENTIFICATION: Two colour phases — female and male. Colour and sex changes occur at 25–30 cm. *Females cream-white with pink upper back and snout; 3 horizontal rows of rectangular, blood-red dashes* on body, 2 originating from eye. *Males have red head and body* with *large cream blotch* on back. Male's dorsal fin red with large, blue-rimmed, black blotch in centre; tail has long upper and lower lobes. Length 50 cm.

DISTRIBUTION: Kermadec Islands; Cape Reinga to East Cape. Most abundant around offshore islands and coastal headlands.

HABITAT: Reefs.

GENERAL: Red pigfish eat a variety of large invertebrates, using their long narrow jaws to prize them from rocks and crevices. At night they rest in holes and crevices. During the July–September spawning season males develop distinctive colour markings, including a white 'V' behind the eye, black shading on the sides, and white upper and lower tail margins. Males court females by arching their bodies around them in tight circles with dorsal and anal fins raised. The male then straddles the female with his pelvic fins, and spawning occurs as the two swim obliquely upwards.

Foxfish (Kotakota) *Bodianus* sp. **Plate 90**

IDENTIFICATION: Only one colour phase known: *red with white lower jaw and belly. Two white spots on back; pectoral fins yellow.* Length 40 cm.

DISTRIBUTION: Cape Reinga to Mahia Peninsula and Cape Egmont. Rarely seen. Usually deeper than 30 m.

HABITAT: Caves and archways on reefs.

GENERAL: Nothing is known of the biology of foxfish.

Combfish *Coris picta* **Plate 91**

IDENTIFICATION: Three colour phases — juvenile, female and male. Juvenile to female colour change occurs at about 8 cm. *Juveniles white with a black stripe* from snout to tip of tail. *Females similar, but tail yellow, and black stripe develops wavy lower edge;* in large females and males, waves expand vertically until black stripe looks like a comb. *Males* same as females, but during courtship and spawning they change within a few seconds to a temporary colour pattern: *black stripe fades to blue-grey* on body but remains dark on head, upper back darkens, and belly becomes yellow-brown. They revert to the 'female' colour pattern after spawning. Length 22 cm.

DISTRIBUTION: Kermadec Islands; Cape Reinga to Aldermen Islands. Rare, most often found around offshore islands.

HABITAT: Reefs with adjacent sand patches.

GENERAL: Combfish of all sizes are cleanerfish, but they also eat free-living crustaceans. They occupy home ranges near sandy areas, suggesting that they sleep under the sand at night, as do the closely related Sandager's wrasse.

Spawning occurs in February–June. During courtship the male swims around the female displaying his fins, and may straddle her as the two swim forwards in an undulating path. Spawning occurs when they swim rapidly upwards. This procedure may be repeated several times before the male reverts to his original colours. Combfish populations are probably maintained by larvae arriving from subtropical regions during warm summers.

Sandager's wrasse *Coris sandageri* **Plates 92–94**

IDENTIFICATION: Three colour phases — juvenile, female and male. Colour changes occur at about 15 cm (juvenile to female) and 30–35 cm (female to male). *Juveniles white with gold stripe* from snout to caudal peduncle; black spot at tail base. *Females cream-white in front, fawn towards rear, with 2 dark brown blotches on sides;* lemon yellow patch on lower side of head. *Males multi-coloured: brown, white and yellow bands on a fawn to mauve body; white, purple and turquoise head.* Males and females have blue-grey fins. Length 50 cm.

DISTRIBUTION: Kermadec Islands; Three Kings Islands to East Cape. Most abundant around offshore islands, but also common along some parts of the mainland coast.

HABITAT: Reefs adjacent to sandy areas.

GENERAL: Sandager's wrasse are very active during the day and are strongly attracted to divers. At dusk they hover over sand patches, then dive beneath a thin layer of sand, where they spend the night. All that is visible of the sleeping fish is a shallow depression in the sand and an occasional puff of water as the gills work. They eat most small animals but prefer brittlestars, chitons and other shellfish, and the eggs of nesting demoiselles and triplefins. Juveniles may clean parasites from other fishes, but they also eat free-living animals.

Males defend territories against each other, particularly during spawning in December–March. During courtship the male displays to a female by raising his dorsal and anal fins; he may then straddle the female, perching on her back with his pelvic fins, while the two swim forwards in an undulating path. Spawning occurs as they swim towards the surface.

Spotty (Paketi, Pakirikiri) *Notolabrus celidotus* Plates 95 and 96

IDENTIFICATION: Two colour phases — female and male. Colour and sex changes occur at 13–19 cm. *Females silver to dark brown (usually yellow-brown) with large brown or black blotch in middle of body;* pelvic and anal fins yellow. Juveniles have same colour pattern as females, but body colour varies with colour of seaweed to provide camouflage. *Males have golden-brown head,* grey-brown body, and a row of *black spots or a black blotch on upper back, with a pale grey band below;* front of dorsal fin yellow; anal fin blue with gold stripe. Length 30 cm.

DISTRIBUTION: Cape Reinga to Stewart Island; Chatham Islands. Abundant throughout its range. Absent from the Three Kings Islands and Snares Islands, where it is replaced by banded wrasse. Endemic.

HABITAT: Ranges from estuaries to reefs. Usually shallower than 10 m. Loose schools of females are sometimes seen swimming in midwater, especially in sheltered waters. Spotties are less abundant in exposed areas than banded wrasse.

GENERAL: Spotties are extremely active by day, but at night they rest in crevices or on a flat bottom in the open, having secreted a mucus coating around their bodies. They eat a wide variety of food; juveniles eat small crustaceans found among the seaweed, whereas adults fossick for crabs, hermit crabs, bivalves, gastropods, brittlestars and worms. Juveniles also clean parasites from other fishes.

Males defend territories against each other, especially during the July–December spawning season. Females occupy home ranges which may overlap with those of other females, and males. Female home ranges are larger than those of males, and both sexes increase the size of their home ranges as they grow. Males court any females passing through their territories by swimming around them at an oblique angle and displaying their dorsal and anal fins. Spawning occurs when a pair swims rapidly towards the surface. Both sexes probably spawn many times during the spawning season.

After a 2-month planktonic larval stage, juveniles about 1.5–2 cm long settle onto the bottom in December–February. They grow rapidly, reaching maturity during their first or second year at a length of 10–15 cm. Sex change occurs at 3–4 years. A few males retain the female colour pattern after changing sex; they do not defend territories, but are able to spawn with females within the territories of other males because of their disguise. Spotties may live at least 7 years.

Girdled wrasse *Notolabrus cinctus* Plates 97 and 98

IDENTIFICATION: Two colour phases — juvenile and adult. Colour change occurs at about 10–15 cm. Both phases have light-brown head with white lower jaw and face, and blue fins. *Juveniles pink-brown with pale band in middle of body. Adults similar, but band is grey or black. Both colour phases appear grey in natural light.* Length 41 cm.

DISTRIBUTION: Three Kings Islands; Hawke Bay and Kapiti Island to Snares Islands; Chatham Islands; Auckland Islands; Campbell Islands. Most abundant in the southern South Island and subantarctic islands; rare north of Cook Strait. Endemic.

HABITAT: Reefs. Usually deeper than 15 m.

1. Hagfish *Eptatretus cirrhatus* (p. 16)

2. Carpet shark *Cephaloscyllium isabellum* (p. 16)

3. Bronze whaler shark *Carcharhinus brachyurus* (p. 17)

4. Eagle ray *Myliobatis tenuicaudatus* (p. 18)

5. Short-tailed stingray *Dasyatis brevicaudata* (p. 17)

6. Long-tailed stingray *Dasyatis thetidis* (p. 17)

8. Mosaic moray *Enchelycore ramosa* (p. 18)

7. Mosaic moray *Enchelycore ramosa* (p. 18)

9. Mottled moray *Gymnothorax prionodon* (p. 19)

10. Speckled moray *Gymnothorax obesus* (p. 19)

11. Yellow moray *Gymnothorax prasinus* (p. 19)

12. Grey moray *Gymnothorax nubilus* (p. 18)

13. Common conger eel
    Conger verreauxi (p. 19)

14. Northern conger eel
    Conger wilsoni (p. 19)

15. Red lizardfish *Synodus doaki* (p. 20)

16. Lavender lizardfish *Synodus similis* (p. 20)

17. Rock cod *Lotella rhacinus* (p. 20)

18. Red cod *Pseudophycis bachus* (p. 20)

19. Southern bastard cod *Pseudophycis barbata* (p. 21)

20. Slender roughy *Optivus elongatus* (p. 22)

21. Common roughy
Paratrachichthys trailli (p. 22)

22. Bigeye *Pempheris adspersus* (p. 34)

23. Golden snapper *Centroberyx affinis* (p. 22)

24. John dory *Zeus faber* (p. 22)

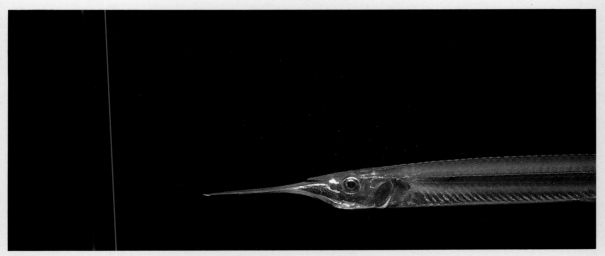

25. Piper *Hyporhamphus ihi* (p. 21)

26. Sea horse *Hippocampus abdominalis* (p. 23)

27. Spiny sea dragon *Solegnathus spinosissimus* (p. 23)

28. Southern pigfish *Congiopodus leucopaecilus* (p. 25)

29. Red gurnard *Chelidonichthys kumu* (p. 25)

30. Northern scorpionfish *Scorpaena cardinalis* (p. 24)

31. Dwarf scorpionfish *Scorpaena papillosus* (p. 25)

32. Sea perch *Helicolenus percoides* (p. 24)

33. Toadstool grouper *Trachypoma macracanthus* (p. 28)

34. Butterfly perch *Caesioperca lepidoptera* (p. 26)

35. Red-lined perch *Lepidoperca tasmanica* (p. 28)

36. Yellow-banded perch *Acanthistius cinctus* (p. 26)

37. Gold-ribbon grouper *Aulacocephalus temmincki* (p. 26)

38. Pink maomao *Caprodon longimanus* (p. 26)

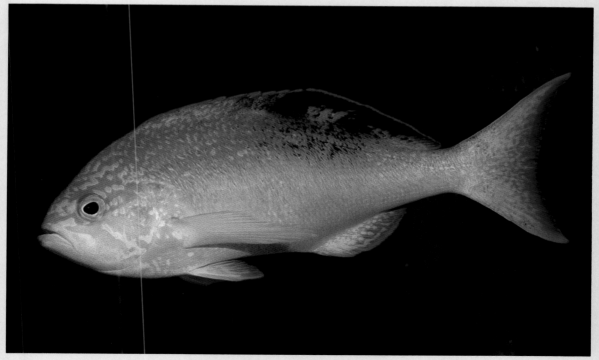

39. Pink maomao (rare colour variety) *Caprodon longimanus* (p. 26)

40. Northern splendid perch, male (top) and female *Callanthias australis* (p. 29)

41. Northern splendid perch
(spawning male)
Callanthias australis (p. 29)

42. Southern splendid perch
Callanthias allporti (p. 28)

43. Red-banded perch *Hypoplectrodes huntii* (p. 27)

44. Half-banded perch *Hypoplectrodes* sp. (p. 28)

45. Spotted black grouper *Epinephelus daemelii* (p. 27)

46. Hapuku *Polyprion oxygeneios* (p. 29)

47. Koheru *Decapterus koheru* (p. 30)

48. Jack mackerel *Trachurus novaezelandiae* (p. 31)

49. Trevally *Pseudocaranx dentex* (p. 30)

50. Kingfish *Seriola lalandi* (p. 30)

51. Kahawai *Arripis trutta* (p. 31)

52. Mado *Atypichthys latus* (p. 37)

53. Snapper *Pagrus auratus* (p. 32)

54. Bar-tailed goatfish *Upeneus francisi* (p. 34)

55. Black-spot goatfish *Parupeneus spilurus* (p. 33)

56. Goatfish *Upeneichthys lineatus* (p. 33)

57. Grey drummer *Kyphosus bigibbus* (p. 34)

58. Silver drummer *Kyphosus sydneyanus* (p. 34)

59. Bluefish *Girella cyanea* (p. 35)

60. Parore *Girella tricuspidata* (p. 35)

61. Grey knifefish *Bathystethus cultratus* (p. 36)

62. Blue knifefish *Labracoglossa nitida* (p. 36)

63. Sweep *Scorpis lineolatus* (p. 36)

64. Blue maomao *Scorpis violaceus* (p. 36)

65. Lord Howe coralfish *Amphichaetodon howensis* (p. 37)

66. Striped boarfish *Evistias acutirostris* (p. 37)

67. Giant boarfish, male (rear) and female *Paristiopterus labiosus* (p. 38)

68. Long-finned boarfish *Zanclistius elevatus* (p. 38)

69. Demoiselle (adult) *Chromis dispilus* (p. 38)

70. Demoiselle (juvenile) *Chromis dispilus* (p. 38)

71. Yellow demoiselle *Chromis fumea* (p. 39)

72. Single-spot demoiselle *Chromis hypsilepis* (p. 39)

73. Black angelfish (adult) *Parma alboscapularis* (p. 39)

74. Black angelfish (juvenile) *Parma alboscapularis* (p. 39)

75. Hiwihiwi *Chironemus marmoratus* (p. 40)

76. Marblefish *Aplodactylus arctidens* (p. 41)

77. Notch-head marblefish *Aplodactylus etheridgii* (p. 41)

78. Painted moki *Cheilodactylus ephippium* (p. 41)

79. Red moki *Cheilodactylus spectabilis* (p. 42)

80. Porae *Nemadactylus douglasii* (p. 42)

81. Tarakihi *Nemadactylus macropterus* (p. 43)

82. Blue moki *Latridopsis ciliaris* (p. 43)

83. Copper moki *Latridopsis forsteri* (p. 44)

84. Trumpeter *Latris lineata* (p. 44)

85. Telescopefish *Mendosoma lineatum* (p. 44)

86. Elegant wrasse (male) *Anampses elegans* (p. 46)

87. Elegant wrasse (female) *Anampses elegans* (p. 46)

88. Red pigfish (male) *Bodianus unimaculatus* (p. 46)

89. Red pigfish (female) *Bodianus unimaculatus* (p. 46)

90. Foxfish *Bodianus* sp. (p. 46)

91. Combfish *Coris picta* (p. 47)

92. Sandager's wrasse (male) *Coris sandageri* (p. 47)

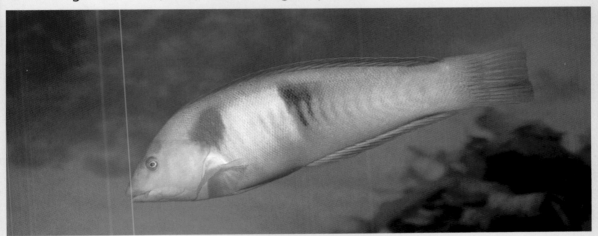

93. Sandager's wrasse (female) *Coris sandageri* (p. 47)

94. Sandager's wrasse (juvenile) *Coris sandageri* (p. 47)

95. Spotty (male) *Notolabrus celidotus* (p. 48)

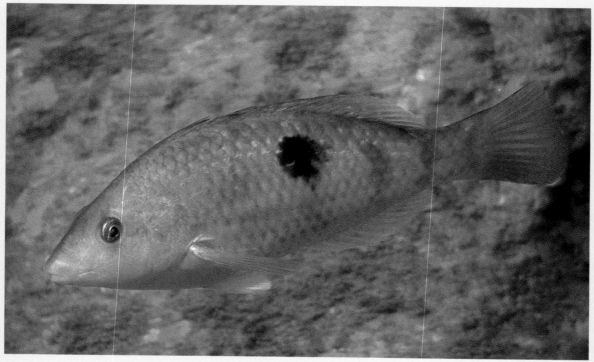

96. Spotty (female) *Notolabrus celidotus* (p. 48)

97. Girdled wrasse (adult) *Notolabrus cinctus* (p. 48)

98. Girdled wrasse (juvenile) *Notolabrus cinctus* (p. 48)

99. Banded wrasse (terminal phase) *Notolabrus fucicola* (p. 49)

100. Banded wrasse (initial phase) *Notolabrus fucicola* (p. 49)

101. Green wrasse (male) *Notolabrus inscriptus* (p. 49)

102. Green wrasse (female) *Notolabrus inscriptus* (p. 49)

103. Orange wrasse (male) *Pseudolabrus luculentus* (p. 50)

104. Orange wrasse (female) *Pseudolabrus luculentus* (p. 50)

105. Scarlet wrasse (male) *Pseudolabrus miles* (p. 50)

106. Scarlet wrasse (female) *Pseudolabrus miles* (p. 50)

107. Rainbowfish (male)
Suezichthys arquatus (p. 50)

108. Rainbowfish (female)
Suezichthys arquatus (p. 50)

109. Crimson cleanerfish (male)
Suezichthys aylingi (p. 51)

110. Crimson cleanerfish (female)
Suezichthys aylingi (p. 51)

111. Blue-finned butterfish (female)
    Odax cyanoallix (p. 51)

112. Butterfish (male)
    Odax pullus (p. 52)

113. Butterfish (female) *Odax pullus* (p. 52)

114. Thornfish *Bovichtus variegatus* (p. 53)

115. Thornfish *Bovichtus variegatus* (p. 53)

116. Maori chief *Notothenia angustata* (p. 53)

117. Small-scaled notothenid *Notothenia microlepidota* (p. 53)

118. Spotted stargazer *Genyagnus monopterygius* (p. 54)

119. Giant stargazer *Kathetostoma giganteum* (p. 54)

120. Blue cod (blue phase) *Parapercis colias* (p. 55)

121. Blue cod (brown phase) *Parapercis colias* (p. 55)

122. Blue cod (juvenile) *Parapercis colias* (p. 55)

123. Opalfish *Hemerocoetes monopterygius* (p. 54)

124. Variable triplefin *Forsterygion varium* (p. 56)

125. Variable triplefin (spawning male) *Forsterygion varium* (p. 56)

126. Spotted triplefin *Grahamina capito* (p. 57)

127. Common triplefin *Forsterygion lapillum* (p. 56)

128. Common triplefin (spawning male) *Forsterygion lapillum* (p. 56)

129. Banded weedfish *Ericentrus rubrus* (p. 59)

130. Yellow-black triplefin *Forsterygion flavonigrum* (p. 56)

131. Yellow-black triplefin (spawning male) *Forsterygion flavonigrum* (p. 56)

132. Oblique-swimming triplefin *Obliquichthys maryannae* (p. 58)

133. Mottled triplefin *Forsterygion malcolmi* (p. 56)

134. Scaly-headed triplefin *Karalepis stewarti* (p. 57)

135. Spectacled triplefin *Ruanoho whero* (p. 58)

136. Yaldwyn's triplefin *Notoclinops yaldwyni* (p. 58)

137. Yaldwyn's triplefin (spawning male) *Notoclinops yaldwyni* (p. 58)

138. Long-finned triplefin *Ruanoho decemdigitatus* (p. 58)

139. Blue-eyed triplefin *Notoclinops segmentatus* (p. 57)

140. Blue-eyed triplefin (spawning male) *Notoclinops segmentatus* (p. 57)

141. Blue-dot triplefin *Notoclinops caerulepunctus* (p. 57)

142. Crested blenny *Parablennius laticlavius* (p. 59)

143. Mimic blenny *Plagiotremus tapeinosoma* (p. 59)

144. Eye-stripe surgeonfish (juvenile) *Acanthurus dussumieri* (p. 60)

145. Spotted sawtail *Prionurus maculatus* (p. 60)

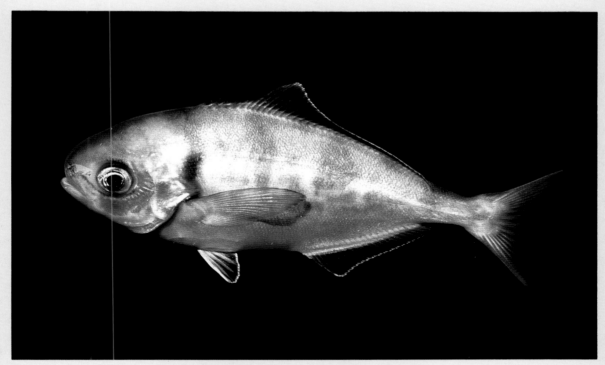

146. Common warehou (juvenile) *Seriolella brama* (p. 60)

147. Yellow-eyed mullet *Aldrichetta forsteri* (p. 45)

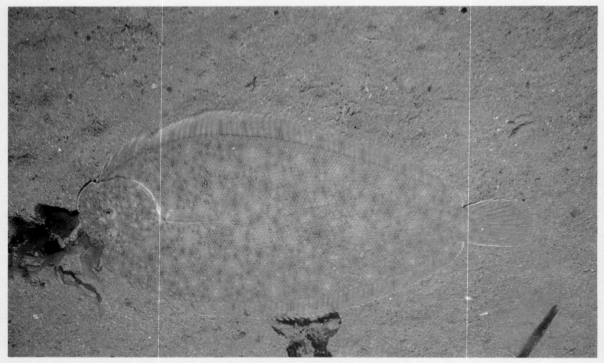

148. Common sole *Peltorhamphus novaezeelandiae* (p. 61)

149. Sand flounder *Rhombosolea plebeia* (p. 61)

150. Leatherjacket (male) *Parika scaber* (p. 62)

151. Leatherjacket (female) *Parika scaber* (p. 62)

152. Clown toado *Canthigaster callisterna* (p. 62)

153. Porcupinefish *Allomycterus jaculiferus* (p. 63)

GENERAL: Girdled wrasse are very active by day, and are inquisitive, approaching divers closely. They eat shellfish, crabs, whalefeed, worms, and planktonic crustaceans. Sex change occurs at about 22–28 cm, and is apparently not accompanied by a colour change. Spawning occurs in summer.

Banded wrasse (Tāngahangaha) *Notolabrus fucicola* Plates 99 and 100

IDENTIFICATION: Two colour phases — initial and terminal. Colour and sex changes occur over a wide length range of 15–30 cm. *Initial phase fish, which may be male or female, usually green or brown with row of yellow spots along back and scattered yellow spots on body.* Juveniles similar in colour, but basic colour can also be golden-brown or red, depending on colour of seaweed in which they are hiding. *Terminal phase fish, nearly always males, blue-grey with yellow blaze on snout, yellow nape band, and 6 cream-yellow spots along back.* Dorsal and anal fins streaked with yellow. Light and dark bands sometimes visible on body. Length 50 cm.

DISTRIBUTION: Three Kings Islands to Snares Islands; Chatham Islands.

HABITAT: Reefs, usually in areas with luxuriant seaweed cover. Most abundant shallower than 10 m, but large males occur down to 50 m.

GENERAL: Banded wrasse are very active by day, and at night they rest in crevices. They eat any small invertebrates such as limpets, chitons, crabs, mussels and small sea urchins.

Unlike other wrasses, many banded wrasse mature as males without passing through a female phase; conversely, many females never change sex to become males. Thus, very small males and very large females may be found. Banded wrasse are also unusual in that a high proportion of fish in the initial colour phase (about 40 percent) are males.

Males defend territories from each other, and court passing females by displaying their dorsal and anal fins; their yellow spots also appear brighter during courtship and the body bands may become more distinct. Spawning occurs during July–December and juveniles 3–4 cm long are found hiding in the seaweed during January–February. They grow rapidly, reaching 12 cm at the end of their first year, and mature during their second year at about 18 cm. Banded wrasse may live for 20 years.

Green wrasse *Notolabrus inscriptus* Plates 101 and 102

IDENTIFICATION: Three colour phases — juvenile, female and male. Colour changes occur at 15–20 cm (juvenile to female) and 24–32 cm (female to male). *Juveniles brown with 10–12 cream-yellow stripes* which break into dashes on rear half of body. *Females olive brown with rows of fine white dashes. Males green with yellow dots on each scale; dorsal and anal fins cream; dark blotch at front of dorsal fin.* Length 50 cm.

DISTRIBUTION: Kermadec Islands; Cape Reinga to East Cape. Abundant at the Kermadecs, but uncommon around New Zealand. Found mainly around offshore islands and coastal headlands.

HABITAT: Reefs. Juveniles and females usually stay close to seaweed and boulders, but males may be seen in open water.

GENERAL: Green wrasse eat large invertebrates such as shellfish, crabs and hermit crabs. Large males also eat small fishes such as triplefins. Males aggressively defend their home ranges against each other, using their spectacular dorsal and anal fins as a warning display. They also display these fins to attract females. Some females never change sex and grow to the size of large males.

Orange wrasse *Pseudolabrus luculentus*
Plates 103 and 104

IDENTIFICATION: Two colour phases — female and male. Colour and sex changes occur at 15–20 cm. *Females yellow-orange with several rows of silver-edged scales along belly,* and silver stripes on lower face; often *light and dark bands along back;* dorsal and anal fins yellow. *Males pink-orange with row of black and white blotches along back;* forehead greenish; dorsal and anal fins red. Length 25 cm. Females differ from female crimson cleanerfish (Plate 110) in having a deeper body and lacking a black dorsal fin spot.

DISTRIBUTION: Kermadec Islands; Three Kings Islands to East Cape. Abundant at Kermadecs but uncommon in New Zealand, where they are usually found around offshore islands and coastal headlands.

HABITAT: Reefs.

GENERAL: Orange wrasse eat small crustaceans and hermit crabs. Juveniles and small females may act as cleanerfish. Males are aggressive towards each other, and other wrasses, particularly during the March–October spawning season. Courtship and spawning occur in pairs or groups. Juveniles grow rapidly and mature during their first year.

Scarlet wrasse (Pūwaiwhakarua)
Pseudolabrus miles **Plates 105 and 106**

IDENTIFICATION: Three colour phases — juvenile, female and male. Colour changes occur at about 6–8 cm (juvenile to female) and 15–30 cm (female to male). *All phases have prominent triangular black wedge in front of tail, and scarlet head* with white lower jaw and throat. Juveniles pale pink-orange above, usually with faint banding; white below. *Females red above, yellow and red striped below. Males have scarlet margin on each scale, making whole body appear scarlet.* Males, and to a less extent females, have elongated upper and lower tail lobes. Length 40 cm. Differs from other wrasses in having black tail wedge.

DISTRIBUTION: Three Kings Islands to Snares Islands; Chatham Islands. Abundant at Three Kings and in the southern part of its range. Endemic.

HABITAT: Reefs, near boulders and crevices. Most abundant below 15 m.

GENERAL: Scarlet wrasse are always moving when in the open but are frequently found sheltering under boulders or in crevices. They eat hermit crabs, crabs, shellfish, brittlestars and sea urchins. Juveniles and females occasionally act as cleanerfish. Spawning occurs in August–November, and juveniles about 5 cm long are found in February–March in shallow water. They grow rapidly, maturing at 1 year old. Females breed for 2–3 years before changing sex at about 4 years old.

Rainbowfish *Suezichthys arquatus* **Plates 107 and 108**

IDENTIFICATION: Two colour phases — female and male. Colour and sex changes occur at about 8–10 cm. *Females pink-orange with about 10 rows of mauve or pink dots* on body; black dots at front and rear of dorsal fin, and at front of tail; body may be banded above. *Males rainbow-coloured with 10 rows of mauve or blue dots,* some of which coalesce into stripes. Dorsal and anal fins red; tail mainly red with triangular green and yellow wedge on upper rear corner. Length 18 cm.

DISTRIBUTION: Kermadec Islands; Cape Reinga to Bay of Plenty. Abundant at the Kermadecs but rare in New Zealand.

HABITAT: Sandy areas adjacent to reefs.

GENERAL: Rainbowfish appear to form stable male-female pairs which are home-ranging. Males court females by raising their dorsal and anal fins, and by undulating the entire body. Spawning probably occurs during winter–spring. Rainbowfish are subtropical immigrants that arrive in northern New Zealand as larvae during warm summers.

Crimson cleanerfish *Suezichthys aylingi*
Plates 109 and 110

IDENTIFICATION: Two colour phases — female and male. Colour and sex changes occur at about 9–10 cm. *Females orange-yellow with several rows of silver scales on belly, and silver stripe on lower face;* one black spot at rear of dorsal fin; tail has blue or clear half-moon in centre; light and dark bands may occur on back. *Males crimson with central silver stripe;* blue lines on head; tail yellow or orange. Length 16 cm. Females differ from female orange wrasse (Plate 104) in being more slender and in having a black dorsal fin spot.

DISTRIBUTION: Kermadec Islands; Three Kings Islands to East Cape. Rare at the Kermadecs, abundant at the Three Kings and common around some offshore islands.

HABITAT: Reefs, often near a rock–sand boundary.

GENERAL: Some crimson cleanerfish feed exclusively on parasites which they remove from larger fishes. Others rarely act as cleanerfish, feeding instead on free-living crustaceans. Males defend permanent territories and maintain harems of up to 10 females. During courtship males display their fins to females and undulate their bodies. Spawning occurs repeatedly during June–December. In January–February juveniles 1 cm long settle onto the reef where they shelter among seaweed. They mature after 7 months, at a length of 7 cm, and reach 10 cm at the end of their first year. They spend 1 or 2 spawning seasons as females, then in February–March many change simultaneously into males, taking about 2 weeks to do so. The new males then compete with each other, and with older males, to establish new territories; many die during this period. Crimson cleaners live a maximum of 4 years.

FAMILY ODACIDAE: Butterfishes

Small to medium, herbivorous or carnivorous, demersal fishes with slender bodies. Butterfishes have teeth fused into sharp cutting plates, which they use for shearing off seaweed. Two species occur in New Zealand.

Blue-finned butterfish *Odax cyanoallix*
Plate 111

IDENTIFICATION: Two colour phases — male and female. Sex and colour changes occur at about 30 cm. *Females yellow-brown with black speckling and irregular white or fawn blotches; silver spot at upper corner of gill cover. Males have same blotchy pattern, but are olive green; bright blue stripes on head; dorsal and anal fins have blue margins.* Length 35 cm. Differs from butterfish (Plates 112 and 113) in colour pattern.

DISTRIBUTION: Three Kings Islands to Poor Knights Islands. Abundant at the Three Kings, common near Cape Reinga, rare elsewhere. Endemic.

HABITAT: Seaweed-covered reefs.

GENERAL: Blue-finned butterfish are almost

totally restricted to the Three Kings Islands, where they replace the ordinary butterfish. They swim by beating their pectoral fins, unlike the ordinary butterfish which swims with an undulating body motion. Blue-finned butterfish are herbivorous, eating mainly kelp. At night they rest in the seaweed forests.

Males are uncommon and are difficult to approach. They occupy large territories and spend much of their time defending them against other males, and courting the many females that live in them. Aggressive and courtship displays involve raising the large dorsal and anal fins. Blue-finned butterfish probably spawn several times during the winter–spring breeding season. Juveniles grow to 10–15 cm after 1 year, and about 20–25 cm after 2 years. They mature first as females during their third year, and after 1 or 2 spawning seasons change into males at about 30 cm length.

Butterfish (Greenbone, Mararī, Kōeaea)
Odax pullus **Plates 112 and 113**

IDENTIFICATION: Several colour phases. Sex change from female to male occurs at about 40 cm. *Juveniles have very slender, golden yellow body with line of silver dashes from snout to caudal peduncle. Females have deeper body than juveniles and are darker above* (brown, olive green or dark green). *Males dark olive green to black above and olive green below; covered with blue dots and wavy blue lines.* Light band along side may be absent from face. *Males have greatly elongated dorsal and anal fins.* During the breeding season both sexes have a bright blue stripe along lower jaw and face. These three colour phases grade into each other, making it sometimes difficult to determine the sex of a fish. Length 70 cm. Differs from blue-finned butterfish (Plate 111) in colour pattern.

DISTRIBUTION: Cape Reinga to Snares Islands; Chatham Islands; Antipodes Islands; Bounty Islands. Most abundant south of Cook Strait. Endemic.

HABITAT: Seaweed-covered reefs. Usually shallower than 20 m.

GENERAL: Adult butterfish eat a variety of large brown seaweeds. They nip off the small reproductive branches of some species, and bite circular discs out of the blades of others. The seaweed is then macerated by teeth in the pharynx before being swallowed. Juveniles eat mainly red seaweeds, but also consume brown seaweeds, crustaceans and gastropods. Feeding activity of all sizes of butterfish peaks in early morning. Butterfish may scull around with their pectoral, dorsal and anal fins when feeding, but usually swim by undulating the body. Juveniles are extremely well camouflaged for hiding among seaweed, and take shelter there if disturbed. Adults swim away if startled.

Male butterfish often occur below about 15 m, whereas females are most common shallower than 10 m. Males establish territories during the breeding season, and defend them against each other with displays of their large dorsal and anal fins. Spawning lasts from July to February, with activity peaking in September–October. Each fish probably spawns many times during the season. Small juveniles settle out of the plankton in 1–2 metres of turbulent water, where they are less likely to be seen by predators. They begin life as females, and reach maturity at 35–40 cm after 4–5 years. Some change sex at about 40 cm after 1 or 2 seasons as females. The oldest males are probably over 10 years old.

FAMILY BOVICHTIDAE: Thornfishes

Small, demersal, carnivorous fishes. Two species occur in coastal waters, but one of them (*Bovichtus psychrolutes*) occurs only at the Snares Islands and the subantarctic islands.

Thornfish *Bovichtus variegatus* **Plates 114 and 115**

IDENTIFICATION: *Variably coloured: ranging from black, through green to brown or red; usually densely mottled with lighter colours, especially cream.* Fins may be yellow or cream with rows of red spots. *Long spine at upper corner of gill cover.* Length 25 cm.

DISTRIBUTION: East Cape and Cape Egmont to Snares Islands; Chatham Islands; Auckland Islands; Campbell Islands. Most abundant in the south, rare north of Cook Strait. Endemic.

HABITAT: Reefs, in rockpools and subtidally in exposed localities.

GENERAL: Thornfish are very well camouflaged, and are often seen only as fast-moving shapes after they have been disturbed. They are usually seen resting on their large pectoral and pelvic fins on rock walls and in crevices. They eat crabs, shrimps and worms. Males grow larger than females, and defend territories from each other.

FAMILY NOTOTHENIIDAE: Antarctic cods

Medium to large, carnivorous, mainly demersal fishes with large flattened heads. Some species have pelagic juveniles. Three species occur in New Zealand.

Maori chief *Notothenia angustata* **Plate 116**

IDENTIFICATION: *Dark olive green to black, covered with pale marbling, giving a tattooed appearance;* base of pectoral fins yellow; belly cream or yellow. Large individuals with *heavy ridges above eyes; scales large.* Length 60 cm. Differs from black cod (not illustrated) and small-scaled notothenid (Plate 117) in its tattooed appearance and presence of eye ridges. Also differs from black cod in size, and from small-scaled notothenid in scale size.

DISTRIBUTION: Cook Strait to Snares Islands; Chatham Islands; and all subantarctic islands. Most common at the subantarctic islands.

HABITAT: Reefs, near caves and crevices.

GENERAL: Maori chiefs are secretive, and are usually seen lying among rocks and weed, where they are well camouflaged. They eat small fishes, crabs and other crustaceans. Some have been found full of seaweed, but it is not known whether this is an important part of their diet.

Small-scaled notothenid *Notothenia microlepidota* **Plate 117**

IDENTIFICATION: *Dark blue, green or purple-brown above, grey below;* throat, gill membranes and base of pectoral fins yellowish. Scales small. Juveniles silver. Length 65 cm. Differs from Maori chief (Plate 116) in lacking tattoos and eye ridges, and from black cod (not illustrated) in size and scale size.

DISTRIBUTION: Otago Peninsula to Snares Islands; Chatham Islands; and all subantarctic islands. Most common at the subantarctic islands.

HABITAT: Reefs. Adults live on the bottom but juveniles school in midwater.

GENERAL: Small-scaled notothenids eat crabs, salps, planktonic crustaceans and fishes. They probably change their diet as they grow, eating mainly pelagic prey as juveniles and demersal prey as adults. Adults are more mobile than Maori chiefs, and are often seen swimming among seaweed.

Black cod *Paranotothenia magellanica* **(not illustrated)**

IDENTIFICATION: Back usually uniform and dark *(black, brown or grey-green),* but may be mottled; belly cream, gold-yellow or reddish; gill membranes orange or red. Pelagic juveniles green-blue above, silver below. *Scales large.* Length 45 cm. Differs from Maori chief (Plate 116) in lacking tattoos and eye ridges, and in size; and from small-scaled notothenid (Plate 117) in size and scale size.

DISTRIBUTION: Kaikoura to Foveaux Strait and all subantarctic islands. Most common at the subantarctic islands and in Otago.

HABITAT: Reefs, near shelter of large rocks.

GENERAL: Juvenile black cod school in midwater, where they feed on plankton. Adults live on the bottom among kelp, and eat mainly crabs, shellfish, small fishes and possibly seaweed; they have also been seen feeding in midwater on swarms of large planktonic crustaceans. They hide under boulders by day, and are rarely seen. Black cod probably spawn in late winter or spring. They mature at 25 cm and 4–5 years, and may live to 9 years.

FAMILY URANOSCOPIDAE:
Armourhead stargazers

Medium to large, carnivorous, demersal fishes with flat, bony heads, eyes on top of the head, and upward-pointing mouths. Stargazers can rapidly dig into mud or sand using their large pectoral fins to excavate a hole and cover themselves. In this pose they are nearly invisible, and are able to lunge out at any prey passing overhead. Two species occur in coastal waters.

Spotted stargazer (Kourepoua) *Genyagnus monopterygius* **Plate 118**

IDENTIFICATION: *Grey, covered with large cream or white spots;* darker band on body at level of pectoral fins. Length 45 cm.

DISTRIBUTION: Cape Reinga to Foveaux Strait. Endemic.

HABITAT: Sand or mud.

GENERAL: Spotted stargazers spend most of their time buried in sand waiting for their prey to pass by. They eat a variety of small fishes and crabs. Spawning occurs in spring and early summer.

Giant stargazer *Kathetostoma giganteum* **Plate 119**

IDENTIFICATION: *Mottled brown or olive green above, often with indistinct stripes along back. Long spine at upper corner of gill cover.* Length 85 cm.

DISTRIBUTION: Cape Reinga to Snares Islands; Chatham Islands; Antipodes Islands; Bounty Islands; Campbell Islands. Endemic.

HABITAT: Sand or mud.

GENERAL: Behaviour and food are as for spotted stargazers. Giant stargazers spawn during winter. Males mature at about 30 cm and females at 40 cm. Females grow larger than males.

FAMILY PERCOPHIDAE: Opalfishes

Small, carnivorous, demersal fishes. One species is likely to be seen in coastal waters.

Opalfish (Kohikohi) *Hemerocoetes monopterygius* **Plate 123**

IDENTIFICATION: *Long slender body; pointed head* with eyes on top. *Dark brown, light brown and white saddles on the back;* belly white; *iridescent orange and blue markings on side of head and along middle of body; margin of anal fin iridescent blue.* Males have elongated upper tail rays. Length 25 cm.

DISTRIBUTION: Cape Reinga to Stewart Island; Chatham Islands. Endemic.

HABITAT: Shell, pebbles and sand.

GENERAL: Opalfish perch on their pelvic and anal fins on the bottom. Their colour provides excellent camouflage against a shelly bottom. They eat crabs, shrimps and small fishes. Opalfish spawn in August–December, and live to 3 years.

FAMILY PINGUIPEDIDAE: Weevers

Small to large, carnivorous, demersal fishes. One species is commonly seen in coastal waters.

Blue cod (Pākirikiri, Rāwaru) *Parapercis colias* Plates 120–122

IDENTIFICATION: Three colour phases. *Juveniles up to about 10 cm white with 2 dark brown or black stripes on back,* one of which continues through eye and onto snout. *In fish 10–25 cm long, stripes fade to light brown* and become less distinct. *Fish over 25 cm blue-grey above with turquoise band behind head,* and white below; tail, upper head and upper lip dark grey. Length 65 cm.

DISTRIBUTION: Three Kings Islands to Snares Islands; Chatham Islands. Most abundant south of Cook Strait. Endemic.

HABITAT: Open reef areas, or sand patches near reefs.

GENERAL: Blue cod are inquisitive and will closely approach divers, frequently biting their fingers or diving gear. They usually swim by sculling their pectoral fins, though they use the tail for short, sharp bursts. They are often seen perched on the bottom

on their large pelvic and pectoral fins. Juveniles eat mainly small crustaceans, but adults eat almost any animal material including shellfish, crustaceans, salps and small fishes.

Large blue cod have large home ranges, and are aggressive towards each other. Tagging experiments have shown that they move around very little, whereas blue cod shorter than about 30 cm move up to 100 km. Blue-phase individuals may be males or females, and although other species in this family change sex this has not been demonstrated in blue cod. Spawning occurs in coastal and outer continental shelf waters from late winter to early summer. Small juveniles about 5 cm long first appear on pebbly or shelly bottom near reef edges in water deeper than 15 m during January–February. As they grow, they gradually move into shallower water. They reach 7–10 cm after 1 year, and mature at 15–25 cm after 2–4 years. Blue cod may live to 17 years.

FAMILY TRIPTERYGIIDAE: Triplefins

Small, carnivorous, demersal fishes (except for the oblique-swimming triplefin which is a schooling species) which have three dorsal fins. Males and females usually have similar colour patterns for much of the year, but during the spawning season males of some species adopt distinctive colours. Triplefins lay eggs in clumps on the bottom, usually on a sloping rock surface. Each nest, which is guarded by the male against predators, may include eggs laid by several females. The male fans the eggs with his fins to aerate them and prevent silt accumulating. After hatching, the larvae become planktonic before settling to the bottom at a length of 1.5–2 cm. Most triplefins are short-lived, reaching a maximum age of about 3 years.

Many species of triplefins are home-ranging, and males defend territories, particularly during the spawning season. They are usually seen perched on their pectoral and pelvic fins. When they swim, they move in short hops.

This is the most diverse family of coastal fishes in New Zealand, comprising at least 25 species. Most are endemic. Many species are poorly known because of their small size and secretive behaviour.

Yellow-black triplefin *Forsterygion flavonigrum* Plates 130 and 131

IDENTIFICATION: *Front of body white with black eyes; black stripe extends halfway along body;* rear half of body yellow or white. In spawning males, body and fins bright yellow, head jet black, and tail usually black. Length 7 cm.

DISTRIBUTION: Three Kings Islands to Snares Islands; Chatham Islands; Auckland Islands. Endemic.

HABITAT: Reefs, particularly on sloping surfaces. Usually deeper than 15 m.

GENERAL: Yellow-black triplefins spawn in June–November, and lay eggs on protected, sloping rock surfaces.

Common triplefin *Forsterygion lapillum* Plates 127 and 128

IDENTIFICATION: Basic body colour varies from white, through grey-brown, to black; *black stripe from above eye to tail* (not visible in black fish); second and third dorsal fins usually red, but may be clear with rows of red dots. Black fish are probably spawning males; they are all black except for white pelvic fins and white anal fin margin. Length 8 cm.

DISTRIBUTION: Cape Reinga to Stewart

Island. Rare at offshore islands. Endemic.

HABITAT: Reefs, particularly areas of cobbles, boulders or rock flats. Most common shallower than 5 m.

GENERAL: Common triplefins spawn during June–January, with activity peaking in August–September. Eggs are laid on smooth rock or coralline paint, particularly on the undersides of cobbles, and they hatch in about 20 days. Juveniles mature at 5 cm after 6 months. Common triplefins probably eat a variety of small invertebrates, and also clean parasites from larger fishes.

Mottled triplefin *Forsterygion malcolmi* Plate 133

IDENTIFICATION: Body pale with *6 irregular red-brown bands; head and pectoral fins yellow to olive-brown;* dorsal fins and tail pink or orange; eye orange. Spawning males blackish, particularly on fins, with white anal fin margin. Length 14 cm.

DISTRIBUTION: Three Kings Islands to Stewart Island; Chatham Islands. Endemic.

HABITAT: Reefs, particularly near boulders or crevices. Most common in depths of 10–25 m.

GENERAL: Mottled triplefins eat shellfish, crustaceans and brittlestars. They spawn in May–August, and lay their eggs on bare rock surfaces such as the sides of boulders. Juveniles settle onto reefs in spring, and grow to 7–8 cm in 6 months.

Variable triplefin *Forsterygion varium* Plates 124 and 125

IDENTIFICATION: *Brown-black blotches along middle of body,* separated by cream-white spots on back; gill covers pink or mauve; belly pale; *eye yellow.* Spawning males grey-black, with light blue margins on anal and first and second dorsal fins. Length 20 cm.

DISTRIBUTION: Three Kings Islands to Snares Islands; Chatham Islands. Rare at offshore islands.

HABITAT: Reefs, particularly broken rock areas with some kelp cover. Most abundant shallower than 10 m.

GENERAL: Variable triplefins eat small crustaceans, crabs, hermit crabs and shellfish. They spawn in May–November with activity peaking in June–July. Eggs are laid on smooth, sloping rock faces, and are guarded by males. Each male may guard up to 9 nests, and females may lay up to 4 batches of eggs during the spawning season. Juveniles grow rapidly to mature at 7–9 cm after 6 months. Males grow faster and bigger than females.

Spotted triplefin *Grahamina capito* **Plate 126**

IDENTIFICATION: *Head and body mottled with dark green;* series of fawn markings along back; dorsal fins and tail have several oblique rows of brown or black dots; anal fin pink or orange with white margin. Length 12 cm.

DISTRIBUTION: Cape Reinga to Snares Islands; Chatham Islands; Antipodes Islands; Auckland Islands. Endemic.

HABITAT: Rock, weed or shell bottom in sheltered bays and estuaries.

GENERAL: Nothing is known of the biology of this species.

Scaly-headed triplefin *Karalepis stewarti* **Plate 134**

IDENTIFICATION: Body variably coloured, but often *fawn with broad, irregular, red or brown bands.* Head mottled red or brown; dorsal and pectoral fins red with rows of yellow spots. Length 20 cm.

DISTRIBUTION: Three Kings Islands to Snares Islands. Endemic.

HABITAT: Reefs, under overhangs and boulders, and in crevices.

GENERAL: Scaly-headed triplefins may be nocturnal, because little activity is seen during the day. They eat small shellfish and crustaceans.

Spawning occurs in June–September, and eggs are laid on the sheltered sides of overhangs and boulders.

Blue-dot triplefin *Notoclinops caerulepunctus* **Plate 141**

IDENTIFICATION: White or transparent; *red or orange spots on head; orange saddles on front of body, and black saddles separated by 7 light blue spots on rear of body;* eyes blue. Length 5 cm.

DISTRIBUTION: Cape Reinga to Stewart Island. Mainly around offshore islands and coastal headlands. Endemic.

HABITAT: Reefs.

GENERAL: Nothing is known of the biology of this species, but it has been seen cleaning parasites from larger reef fishes.

Blue-eyed triplefin *Notoclinops segmentatus* **Plates 139 and 140**

IDENTIFICATION: *Head yellow-orange; body silver with 9 red bands; eyes iridescent blue.* Spawning males have orange head, front of body, and pectoral fins; black bands on rear half of body, and black tail and anal fin. Length 6 cm.

DISTRIBUTION: Cape Reinga to Stewart Island. Endemic.

HABITAT: Reefs, particularly on steep slopes or under overhangs.

GENERAL: Blue-eyed triplefins eat small crustaceans, but have also been seen cleaning parasites from large reef fishes such as moray eels (Plate 12). They spawn in August–January, and lay their eggs in crevices. Juveniles mature at 3–3.5 cm at the end of their first year.

Yaldwyn's triplefin *Notoclinops yaldwyni* **Plates 136 and 137**

IDENTIFICATION: *Pale fawn with many black dots;* eye golden with brown 'teardrop' beneath. Spawning males have grey-green head, bright orange body, and yellow-green margin on first dorsal fin. Length 7 cm.

DISTRIBUTION: Three Kings Islands to Stewart Island; Chatham Islands. Endemic.

HABITAT: Reefs, on steep slopes or overhangs. Usually in turbulent water less than 10 m deep.

GENERAL: Spawning occurs mainly in winter–spring, but may last into late summer some years. Yaldwyn's triplefins lay their eggs on steep rock faces or in crevices.

Oblique-swimming triplefin *Obliquichthys maryannae* **Plate 132**

IDENTIFICATION: *Yellow-orange with black stripe and black eyes. Usually seen in schools of several to thousands of individuals swimming at an oblique angle.* Fish seen near bottom may have pattern of light and dark bands on back, and faint stripe. Length 8 cm.

DISTRIBUTION: Three Kings Islands to Snares Islands. Endemic.

HABITAT: Usually seen swimming up to 5 m above reefs.

GENERAL: Oblique-swimming triplefins are the only triplefins known to form schools. They eat mainly small plankton, which they catch while facing into the current, but are also known to eat bottom-living crustaceans and shellfish. Fish with dark bands on the back may be seen close to the rocks or in crevices during winter. Banded fish collected in September were ripe females, suggesting that the changes in colour pattern and

behaviour are related to spawning. Schools of juveniles 1 cm long appear on reefs in September.

Long-finned triplefin *Ruanoho decemdigitatus* **Plate 138**

IDENTIFICATION: *Females grey, mottled with dark brown, black and cream-yellow;* several fine white lines circle head and gill covers; dorsal, tail and anal fins pink or orange, and anal fin has white margin. Males black, apart from white pelvic fins and white anal fin margin. Length 12 cm.

DISTRIBUTION: Three Kings Islands to Stewart Island; Chatham Islands. Endemic.

HABITAT: Reefs, usually near boulders or crevices. Rarely deeper than 10 m.

GENERAL: Long-finned triplefins spawn during June–October, and lay their eggs on the undersides of flat stones.

Spectacled triplefin *Ruanoho whero* **Plate 135**

IDENTIFICATION: *Body and fins red-brown with light blue oblique lines; appear grey in dim light; eyes and space between them black; several light blue lines circle head and eyes.* Spawning males black, apart from white pelvic fins, white anal fin margin, and grey patches on dorsal fins. Length 12 cm.

DISTRIBUTION: Three Kings Islands to Snares Islands; Chatham Islands. Endemic.

HABITAT: Reefs, usually near the shelter of boulders or crevices.

GENERAL: Spectacled triplefins eat crabs and small crustaceans. They spawn in June–November. Juveniles appear on reefs in September, and mature during their first year.

FAMILY CLINIDAE: Weedfishes

Small, carnivorous, seaweed-dwelling fishes.

Three species occur in New Zealand, but they are rarely seen because of their excellent camouflage.

Banded weedfish (Orange clinid) *Ericentrus rubrus* **Plate 129**

IDENTIFICATION: *Highly variable in colour: may be blue, green, red, yellow, orange-brown or dark brown, mottled and banded with various camouflage colours.* Snout pointed; second dorsal fin very long. Length 11 cm.

DISTRIBUTION: Three Kings Islands to Kaikoura; Chatham Islands. Endemic.

HABITAT: Seaweed. Usually shallower than 15 m.

GENERAL: Banded weedfish are extremely well camouflaged, adapting their colour to match the seaweed. They are rarely seen, but when located they will stay still, darting away only a few centimetres if prodded. They eat small crustaceans found among the seaweed. Banded weedfish mature at about 4 cm, and give birth to live young in summer.

FAMILY BLENNIIDAE: Blennies

Small, carnivorous, demersal fishes, usually with two or more feathery tentacles on the top of the head. Two species occur in New Zealand.

Crested blenny *Parablennius laticlavius* **Plate 142**

IDENTIFICATION: *Large, blunt head with steeply sloping face and small tentacle above each eye.* Back yellow behind head; *body white with dark red to black stripe from eyes to caudal peduncle.* Length 8 cm.

DISTRIBUTION: Kermadec Islands; Three Kings Islands to Cook Strait. Most common in the north.

HABITAT: Reefs, in or near holes or barnacle and tube worm shells. Usually shallower than 20 m.

GENERAL: Crested blennies are often seen resting on a rock face in the open, but will dart into a hole or empty worm tube if frightened. They enter their holes tail-first with a wriggling motion, then sit near the entrance with only the head showing. Crested blennies eat a variety of small animals, including crustaceans, hydroids, barnacle feet, and shellfish and fish eggs. During winter and spring females lay their eggs on the inside of the male's hole, and he guards them until they hatch. Juveniles 1–1.5 cm long appear on the reef during summer.

Mimic blenny *Plagiotremus tapeinosoma* **Plate 143**

IDENTIFICATION: *Very slender, dark green body with 2 silver stripes from snout to caudal peduncle; central dark stripe composed of light and dark bands; underside of head orange; tail yellow. Swims with a sinuous body motion.* Length 8 cm.

DISTRIBUTION: Kermadec Islands; Three Kings Islands to East Cape.

HABITAT: Reefs, in holes or barnacle and worm shells, and swimming in midwater above the reef. Usually shallower than 15 m.

GENERAL: Mimic blennies eat the skin, mucus, scales and fins of other fishes. They use their colour pattern to mimic other small, harmless fishes (especially oblique-swimming triplefins, which they frequently school with), and when close to larger fishes they make a rapid strike at them, nipping a fin or scraping off some mucus with their underslung jaws. This leaves characteristic wavy gouges on the skin of their victims (see Plate 59). Mimic blennies retreat to their holes, which they enter tail-first, if frightened or chased. Females lay their eggs in a male's hole or shell, where he guards them until they hatch.

FAMILY ACANTHURIDAE: Surgeonfishes

Medium to large herbivorous or planktivorous demersal fishes, with sharp spines or bony plates on the caudal peduncle. Two species occur in New Zealand.

Eye-stripe surgeonfish *Acanthurus dussumieri* **Plate 144**

IDENTIFICATION: *Juveniles grey-brown with yellowish dorsal and pectoral fins; front of tail yellow, rear black;* yellow patch around eye. *Spine on caudal peduncle lies in black-rimmed, white socket.* Adults yellow-brown with fine, wavy blue stripes; yellow patch around eye, and yellow stripe between eyes; black gill membrane. Dorsal and anal fins yellow with blue base; tail lunate, yellow at base, otherwise blue with black spots. Peduncle spine as for juveniles. Length 50 cm.

DISTRIBUTION: Cape Reinga to Leigh. Rare.

HABITAT: Rocky reefs.

GENERAL: Only juvenile eye-stripe surgeonfish have so far been recorded in New Zealand. They are tropical immigrants that arrive as larvae during warm summers, but do not survive their first winter. Eye-stripe surgeonfish graze fine seaweed from rocks or sand, and they may also feed on detritus.

Spotted sawtail (Spotted surgeonfish) *Prionurus maculatus* **Plate 145**

IDENTIFICATION: Body oval and head small. *Blue-grey, covered with yellow dots and dashes;* row of short, faint, orange-brown bands on sides. *Three blue keeled plates on each side of caudal peduncle;* often a white saddle above last plate. Fins blue with yellow spots. Juveniles similar except bands on sides are longer and more prominent, and they have few spots. Length 60 cm.

DISTRIBUTION: Kermadec Islands; Cape Reinga to Cook Strait. Rare in New Zealand.

HABITAT: Sheltered reefs. Usually less than 10 m deep.

GENERAL: Spotted sawtails usually occur singly in New Zealand, but in subtropical areas they may form large schools. They are herbivorous, using their small jaws to graze fine seaweed. Spotted sawtails are seen only sporadically, suggesting that they are subtropical immigrants that arrive in northern New Zealand as larvae during warm summers.

FAMILY CENTROLOPHIDAE: Warehou and butterfishes

Medium to large, planktivorous, mainly pelagic fishes. One species occurs in coastal waters.

Common warehou (Warehou) *Seriolella brama* **Plate 146**

IDENTIFICATION: *Blue-grey above, silver below; large black blotch above pectoral fin.* Juveniles have irregular grey blotches over much of body. Length 85 cm.

DISTRIBUTION: Hauraki Gulf and Albatross Point to Snares Islands; Chatham Islands; Antipodes Islands; Bounty Islands. Most abundant south of Cook Strait.

HABITAT: Adults form large schools over the continental shelf, but juveniles are seen in small schools in harbours and bays.

GENERAL: Adult common warehou eat planktonic salps, jellyfish, crustaceans and squid. Juveniles probably eat small crustaceans. Spawning occurs during much of the year, but peaks in winter–spring. Juveniles grow to about 13 cm at the end of their first year, and 50 cm after 5 years. They may live to 17 years.

FAMILY PLEURONECTIDAE: Right-eyed flounders

Small to large, carnivorous, demersal fishes with flattened bodies and both eyes on the right side. Larvae are symmetrical, with one eye on each side, and they swim upright. As they transform into juveniles and settle to the bottom, the left eye migrates to the right side of the head, and the left side becomes the under-side. In most species the under-side is pale and the upper-side adopts the colour and pattern of the surrounding seabed. Eleven species of right-eyed flounders have been recorded in New Zealand, but only the two most likely to be seen by divers are included here.

Common sole (New Zealand sole, Pātiki rori) *Peltorhamphus novaezeelandiae* Plate 148

IDENTIFICATION: *Oval, green to grey body,* sometimes with up to three dark blotches on lateral line; white below. *Mouth covered by rounded, fleshy flap in front of eyes.* Scales prominent. Length 68 cm. Two other New Zealand species of *Peltorhamphus* are difficult to distinguish, but are less than 20 cm long.

DISTRIBUTION: Cape Reinga to Foveaux Strait; Chatham Islands. Most abundant, and larger, in the south. Endemic.

HABITAT: Sand or mud bottom in estuaries, harbours and bays.

GENERAL: Common soles are easily approached underwater (though difficult to find), because they trust their excellent camouflage to protect them from predators. When disturbed, they swim in rapid bursts with their upper-side pectoral fin raised as a steering oar. After settling, they partially burrow into the sediment by rippling their side fins. Common soles feed at night on worms, crustaceans and small shellfish that live in or on the sand and mud. They are very mobile when searching for food, and may swim in midwater. Common soles spawn over an extended period in winter–spring, with activity peaking in August–September.

Sand flounder (Dab, Pātiki) *Rhombosolea plebeia* Plate 149

IDENTIFICATION: *Diamond-shaped, grey or brown above,* white below. *Mouth visible from above; scales not apparent.* Length 46 cm.

DISTRIBUTION: Cape Reinga to Stewart Island; Chatham Islands. Endemic.

HABITAT: Sand, mud or gravel bottom in estuaries, harbours and bays.

GENERAL: During the day sand flounders lie on the bottom, partially or fully covered with sand or mud. Their camouflage colours provide good protection from predators, and they remain still when approached by divers. Colours and patterns can change dramatically within a few seconds to blend in with a new background. They usually swim by undulating their side fins, but can accelerate rapidly using their tail. Sand flounders feed at night, and are much more active then. They eat a wide variety of crustaceans, worms, brittlestars and small shellfish that live in or on the mud and sand. Large amounts of mud and detritus, and some seaweeds, are also ingested while feeding.

In the north, sand flounders have a long spawning period from March to December.

In the south, spawning is mainly confined to spring. Soon after their transformation to the juvenile stage, sand flounders settle to the seabed and migrate to mud flats in bays, harbours and estuaries, and may even enter rivers. They remain in the shallows until they are 2 years old, when they migrate to spawning grounds in deeper water (30–50 m). Thereafter they migrate backwards and forwards to shallow water in spring–summer, and spawning grounds in autumn–winter.

Males mature at about 10 cm, and reach 15–17 cm at 2 years of age. Females grow faster than males, maturing at 16–20 cm and reaching 23–24 cm at 2 years. Females average more than 30 cm long at 3 years. Few sand flounders live longer than 4 years.

FAMILY MONACANTHIDAE:
Leatherjackets

Small to medium, carnivorous, demersal or pelagic fishes with diamond-shaped bodies, strong first dorsal spines and small mouths. One species is commonly seen in coastal waters.

Leatherjacket (Kōkiri) *Parika scaber* **Plates 150 and 151**

IDENTIFICATION: *Distinctive body shape and dorsal spine* (usually raised when approached closely). Body varies from almost white to dark brown; spots on body and stripes on head may be present or absent. Males have yellow-green tail with fine black band near rear edge; females have grey-brown tail. Other fins usually yellow. Courting males have dark grey head; body may be light grey (almost white) or dark grey with light blotches. Length 45 cm.

DISTRIBUTION: Kermadec Islands; Three Kings Islands to Stewart Island; Chatham Islands.

HABITAT: Reefs, sand and midwater.

GENERAL: Leatherjackets can swim either forwards or backwards by undulating their dorsal and anal fins; the tail is rarely used. They eat almost any living matter (mainly sponges and ascidians) which they graze at right angles to the rock. They sometimes aggregate in midwater to feed on salps and jellyfish.

A raised dorsal spine, spread tail fan and contrasting colour pattern are used by males during the August–November spawning season as a signal to attract females and repel other males. Eggs are laid in nests on the bottom, but they are not guarded by the adults. The eggs hatch into planktonic larvae, and in early summer golden-brown juveniles less than 1 cm long settle to the bottom and hide in kelp. They grow to 10 cm after only 4 months, during which time they gradually move out into more open habitat. Leatherjackets mature at 19–22 cm and an age of 2 years, and may live for over 7 years.

FAMILY TETRAODONTIDAE:
Pufferfishes

Small to medium, carnivorous fishes with a variety of lifestyles. They have a beak of fused teeth, and can inflate themselves with water for protection from predators. All species are poisonous. One species is likely to be seen by divers.

Clown toado (Sharp-nosed puffer) *Canthigaster callisterna* **Plate 152**

IDENTIFICATION: *Olive brown or green above, white below, with 2 dark stripes through middle of body;* whole body covered in *wavy blue lines and dots* which fade on belly; dorsal and anal fins blue and yellow striped; *tail has brown stripes along upper and lower margins,* and rows of blue dots in centre. Length 20 cm.

DISTRIBUTION: Kermadec Islands; Cape Reinga to East Cape. Most common around offshore islands and coastal headlands.

HABITAT: Reefs, often near a boundary with sand, pebbles or boulders. Usually deeper than 10 m.

GENERAL: Clown toados eat a variety of encrusting animals (sponges, bryozoans, ascidians) and small crustaceans. They swim by undulating their dorsal and anal fins, but use the tail for rapid bursts of speed. Males probably grow bigger than females, and defend territories against each other. They display to each other by spreading their colourful tail fans. Spawning probably occurs in winter or spring, and juveniles first appear on reefs in summer and autumn.

FAMILY DIODONTIDAE:
Porcupinefishes

Medium to large, carnivorous fishes with a variety of lifestyles. They have numerous spines embedded in the skin; these become erect when they inflate themselves with water as a protection against predators. One species occurs in New Zealand.

Porcupinefish (Kōpūtōtara) *Allomycterus jaculiferus* **Plate 153**

IDENTIFICATION: *Body covered with spines, largest on back and caudal peduncle; dorsal and anal fins at rear. Green, grey or brown above, with black and yellow blotches centred on some spines; white below.* Length 60 cm.

DISTRIBUTION: Three Kings Islands to Foveaux Strait. Most abundant north of Cook Strait.

HABITAT: Forms large schools over open bottom, occasionally seen singly over reefs.

GENERAL: Porcupinefish are uncommon over reefs, but those seen there often stay in the same place for several weeks or longer. They swim by sculling their dorsal and anal fins, but use the tail for rapid bursts of speed. When in danger they inflate themselves with water, causing the spines in the skin to become even more erect. In this state they are virtually inedible for any predator. Porcupinefish have powerful jaws of fused teeth which they use to crush hard-shelled invertebrates such as shellfish, sea urchins and crabs. They probably spawn in summer.

Glossary

Claspers A pair of rod-like structures, made of cartilage, which are attached to the pelvic fins of male sharks and rays (see Plate 2). They are used for transferring sperm during mating.

Crustaceans An extremely important group of invertebrate animals which have hard, jointed, external skeletons. There are numerous marine species, including minute planktonic animals, krill, shrimps, barnacles, crabs and crayfish.

Demersal Living on or near the seabed.

Fish(es) I use the words 'fish' and 'fishes' here to include sharks, rays and bony fishes. The plural of 'fish' can be either 'fish' or 'fishes' in everyday language. I have used 'fishes' for more than one species of fish, and 'fish' for more than one individual fish of the same species.

Home range An area inhabited by a fish for a reasonable period of its life.

Invertebrates Animals without backbones. In the sea, this term applies to all animals except fishes, turtles, sea snakes and marine mammals (whales, dolphins and seals).

Pelagic Living in open water, away from the seabed.

Planktivorous Fishes that eat plankton.

Plankton Microscopic to small plants and animals that live in open water, and have limited powers of locomotion. Many fishes go through planktonic stages as eggs or larvae, but fishes that live in open water as adults are usually considered pelagic rather than planktonic.

Species A group of animals or plants capable of interbreeding, and of producing fertile offspring. (Hybrids between species are usually sterile.) The word 'species' is both singular and plural.

Spiracles The openings of a pair of tubes that connect the back of the head (behind the eyes) with the throat in sharks and rays (see Plates 5 and 6). They are used for taking in water for breathing while the mouth is closed. They are large in rays, which spend much of their lives lying on the seabed.

Territory A home range that is actively defended, usually against other fish of the same species and sex.

Photograph credits and locations

Photographers

T. Ayling   Plates 91, 108, 142
Q. Bennett 8, 61
W. Farrelly 13, 14, 24, 27, 41
R. Grace 3, 44, 55, 104
K. Grange 35
L. Hellyer 80
R. Kuiter 114, 128, 146
D. Maddox 68, 130
G. Osborne 116
J. Randall 54
L. Ritchie 6, 15, 16, 90, 112, 152
L. Shaw 83
D. Torckler 67
K. Westerskov 5, 18, 25, 46, 85, 97, 115, 117, 119
M. Williams 2, 111, 125, 127, 132, 139, 140

All other photographs were taken by the author.

Locations

Norfolk Island   Plates 33, 36, 50, 54, 71, 77, 78
Lord Howe Island   86, 87, 145
Australia   146

All other photographs were taken in New Zealand.

Further reading

Ayling, T. & Cox, G.J. *Collins Guide to the Sea Fishes of New Zealand*. Collins, Auckland, 1982.

Doak, W. *Fishes of the New Zealand Region*. Hodder & Stoughton, Auckland, 1972.

Doak, W. *Wade Doak's World of New Zealand Fishes*. Hodder & Stoughton, Auckland, 1991.

Graham, D.H. *A Treasury of New Zealand Fishes*. Reed, Wellington, 1956 (2nd ed.).

Paul, L. *New Zealand Fishes: An Identification Guide*. Reed Methuen, Auckland, 1986.

Paulin, C. & Roberts, C. *The Rockpool Fishes of New Zealand*. Museum of New Zealand Te Papa Tongarewa, Wellington, 1992.

Paulin, C., Stewart, A., Roberts C., & McMillan, P. *New Zealand Fish: A Complete Guide*. National Museum of New Zealand Miscellaneous Series 19, 1989.

Index